SAINSBURY'S RECIPE LIBRARY

RICE, BEANS
& PASTA

SAINSBURY'S RECIPE LIBRARY

RICE, BEANS & PASTA

ROZ DENNY

CONTENTS

Published exclusively for J Sainsbury plc
Stamford House Stamford Street
London SE1 9LL
by Martin Books
Simon & Schuster Consumer Group
Grafton House, 64 Maids Causeway
Cambridge CB5 8DD

ISBN 0 85941 827 8
First published 1986
Paperback edition 1992
© Woodhead-Faulkner (Publishers) Ltd 1986, 1992
All rights reserved
Printed and bound by Butler & Tanner, Frome, Somerset

INTRODUCTION

Many of the world's oldest and most delicious recipes are based on cereals and pulses. With the current emphasis on healthier eating, rice, pulses and pasta are becoming increasingly popular. They are nutritious, good sources of dietary fibre, and they offer a variety of flavours and textures. The recipes in this book show just how versatile these foods can be.

RICE

The staple food for half of the world, rice is commonly eaten in this country too. Not only is it convenient to use, it is a good source of B vitamins, minerals, protein and fibre. Rice provides just 35 calories per 25 g (1 oz) cooked weight. There are many varieties of rice, each with different properties. Some cook to a light separate fluffiness, some to a creamy consistency and others to a sticky mass suitable for moulding. Choosing the right rice for a dish is essential.

Long-grain rice

This cooks as separate grains. Most long-grain rice sold in this country is the Patna type, now grown mainly in America. For white rice, the outer husk and bran layer are removed and it is then milled and 'pearled'. Long-grain brown rice is Patna-type rice with just the outer husk removed. It absorbs more water and takes longer to cook than pearled rice, but it contains more protein and has a better flavour. The best quality long-grain rice available in this country is the aromatic Basmati rice. It is the ideal rice to use in pilafs or to serve with curries. It is more expensive than ordinary long-grain rice, but delicious. Basmati benefits from thorough rinsing in cold water before cooking.

Round-grain rice

These cook to varying degrees of creaminess. Risotto rices, from Northern Italy, are cooked with stock in dishes which are served moist. Brown and white types are available; the best is 'Arborio'. Short-grain, or pudding, rices are creamier still, and are best served soft after absorbing sweetened milk and flavourings.

Easy-cook rice

Also known as par-boiled rice. Some people find it slightly more chewy. It is good served as an accompaniment or in salads.

Glutinous rice

The rice of South-East Asia and Japan. The grains cook to a sticky but still light texture.

To cook long-grain rice

There are two methods; both are quite simple but do require careful timing.
1. Add the rice to a large pan containing plenty of boiling water. Add salt, lower the heat to a brisk simmer and cook for 12 minutes for white rice, 25–30 minutes for brown.

To test if cooked, press a grain between finger and thumb—if it splits in two without a hard core, then it's done. Drain immediately through a colander and rinse under cold water to stop cooking. Toss in a little oil or butter and sprinkle with chopped parsley. Heat through in a steamer or warm oven.

2. This is known as the total absorption method—the rice totally absorbs all of the water. It is the method most suited to easy-cook rice. The general rule is to allow twice the volume of water to rice. So, for example, one teacupful of rice should be cooked with 2 teacupfuls of water.

Place the rice and water (or stock) in a saucepan, add salt to taste, bring to the boil, cover and simmer until cooked; do not lift the lid during this time. Test to see if the rice is cooked (as above). If the rice is cooked but the water not fully absorbed, simmer uncovered for 1–2 minutes. Serve as above.

PULSES

Pulses—dried beans and peas—are rapidly gaining popularity in this country as we begin to appreciate their nutritional value. They contain more protein and B group vitamins than grains and vegetables, plus valuable minerals and dietary fibre. All that—for around 35 calories per 25 g (1 oz) cooked weight.

Pulses yield double their dried weight when cooked, so take this into account when calculating quantities. If you use either ready cooked or canned pulses, use double the dried weight specified in the recipe.

To cook pulses

Nearly all pulses need soaking for at least 8 hours in 4 times the quantity of cold water to help soften the outer skins; if time is short, cover with boiling water and soak for 2 hours. Lentils, split peas and mung beans do not need soaking, but it will shorten the final cooking time if they are.

Drain off the soaking water. Cover with fresh cold water, bring to the boil and boil hard for 10 minutes, then simmer, partially covered, for the given time according to type (see below). Check the water level occasionally and top up with boiling water if necessary. As pulses age, their skins toughen which prolongs the cooking time, so check towards the end of the suggested times. Add salt or lemon juice to taste for the last 5 minutes or while the pulses are draining.

It is most important to ensure that you boil all pulses for 10 minutes, as this destroys the harmful toxins present in them. For the same reason, it is not advisable to cook them in their soaking liquids. Soaking and boiling also help prevent flatulence by breaking down some of the substances which are the cause.

Pressure cooking is an excellent way of cooking pulses and reduces the total time to about a third with cookers at 15 lbs pressure. Check your instruction manual for full details, but generally cook up to 250 g (8 oz) dried weight at a time in about 600 ml (1 pint) water. Do not season, but add about 1 tablespoon oil to cut down on any frothing.

For cooking in slow cookers, soak and boil the beans for 10 minutes as above, before adding to the cooker. Microwave ovens do not cook pulses any quicker than conventional methods.

There are numerous types of pulses available: they come in various shapes, sizes and colours and have different textures, tastes and cooking times.

Aduki beans

Small reddish-brown bean from the Far East. A good nutty flavour and texture and appetizing colour. Useful as a substitute for mince in a dish. Use whole or mashed or a mixture. Good for sprouting too. Simmer for 40 minutes.

Black beans
Popular in South and Central American cuisine. Lovely 'meaty-cum-mushroom' flavour, ideal in soups and stews. Simmer for 50 minutes.

Black eye beans
Small kidney-shaped bean with a distinctive black spot. Good flavour and texture. Nice with rice. Holds shape well when cooked. Can be sprouted, but slightly tricky. Simmer for 50 minutes.

Borlotti beans
Italian pulse, very similar to the kidney bean. Speckled brown, or all brown. Use in place of kidney beans. Simmer for 50 minutes. Available canned.

Broad beans (Fava beans)
Before the discovery of the kidney bean, this was the most popular dried bean in Europe. Now mainly used in Middle Eastern cuisine. Needs pressing out of its skin when cooked. Simmer for 50 minutes.

Butter beans (Lima or Madagascar beans)
Very popular, versatile pulse. Creamy texture, full of flavour. If cooked carefully, holds its shape well. Excellent served simply with butter and chopped parsley. Good cold in salads. Simmer for 1 hour. Available canned.

Cannellini beans (White kidney beans)
A good all-purpose bean with a nice, subtle flavour and firm texture. Popular in Italian cooking and excellent cold. Simmer for 50 minutes. Available canned.

Chick peas (Garbanzos)
Cream-fawn coloured pea with a creamy, nutty flavour and slightly chewy skin. Holds its shape very well. Popular in Middle Eastern, Spanish and Central American cooking. Used in dips, and with spicy foods. A good sprouter. Simmer for 1 hour (skins may seem a little tough, so check by tasting). Available canned.

Flageolet beans
Slimmer, more elegant kidney-shaped bean, pale green in colour. Excellent as a simple accompaniment to lamb. Popular in France. Nice cold with vinaigrette. Simmer for 50 minutes.

Haricot beans (Navy or pea beans)
The original baked bean. Often confused with cannellini beans, but smaller, with a firmer texture and more delicate flavour. Popular in French cooking. *The* bean for cassoulets. Simmer for 50 minutes.

Lentils
A popular pulse with a delicious and versatile flavour. The red lentil is the most common in this country, but the green and brown Continental lentils are now becoming more widely available. Red lentils cook to a thick purée, good for sauces and soups. Continental lentils hold their shape better and have a fuller flavour. The best green lentil is the Puy, much prized in France. Brown Indian lentils (Masoor Dhal) are unsplit red lentils (sometimes mis-named Continental lentils). Continental lentils are good sprouters.

Not necessary to soak, but will help shorten cooking time for green and brown lentils. Simmer for 15–20 minutes for red lentils; 20 minutes for soaked Continental lentils; 50 minutes for unsoaked Continental lentils.

Mung beans
Small, green bean with creamy, nutty flavour. Not necessary to soak, but shortens cooking time. Cook for 25 minutes for soaked mung beans; 40 minutes for unsoaked.

Pinto beans
Speckled pink variety of kidney bean. Often interchangeable in Mexican dishes with red kidney beans. Cook and use as red kidney beans.

Red kidney beans
Now one of the most popular pulses. Good, slightly sweet flavour, firm texture and nice, glossy colour when cooked. Many uses in hot savoury dishes, for refried beans, and cold in salads. Simmer for 1 hour. Available canned.

Soya beans
Highly nutritious and used extensively commercially, but not perhaps the most flavoursome. Soak for 12 hours. Simmer for 2¾ hours.

Split peas
Several types. Most common in this country are yellow and green split peas. Good as an accompaniment, the basis of a main vegetarian meal or in soups. Popular in Indian cooking. Use green split peas for pease pudding, which is traditionally wrapped in muslin and boiled with a bacon or ham joint.

Not necessary to soak, but helps shorten cooking time. Simmer for 15 minutes if soaked; 30 minutes if unsoaked.

Whole peas (Marrow fat)
Round, pale green, full-flavoured pea with a floury texture. Popular as mushy peas. Good for soups, purées, dips and accompaniments for bacon, pork and meat pies. Sprouts well with a crisp texture. Simmer for 1–1¼ hours.

To sprout beans and peas
Fresh home-grown bean sprouts are highly nutritious, a good source of fibre and very digestible. Most beans and peas are suitable for sprouting. They take from 2 to 5 days to germinate and grow to the optimum size for eating, as follows: green and brown lentils 2 days; mung and soya beans 3 days; whole peas, chick peas and aduki beans 3–4 days; and flageolet and haricot beans 3–5 days. They are ready for eating when they are 2 or 3 times their bean length.

Buy beans sold for home sprouting or from a store with a high turnover. If nothing has happened after 48 hours, the beans are probably old and will not sprout.

Follow the instructions below to obtain delicious home-grown bean sprouts; once you have established which sprouts you like and in what quantities you can eat them, keep a few jars going at various stages, for a constant supply.

1. Place 2 or 3 tablespoons beans in a jar and cover with a least 4 times the volume of tepid water.
2. Cover the jar with muslin or cheesecloth and secure with an elastic band. Soak overnight.
3. Drain through the cloth top. Rinse the beans well with tepid water and drain.
4. Turn the jar on its side and shake gently to space out the beans. Place the jar on a tray in a warm room, away from draughts and direct sunlight.
5. Rinse 2 or 3 times a day through the cloth top. Discard any mouldy beans.

Use bean sprouts whenever you want crunch, freshness and flavour. For instance, they can be added to almost any salad, sprinkled over pasta, stirred into croquette or burger mixtures before shaping, used in pilaffs, risottos, fried rice and stuffings—and they make an attractive garnish for many dishes.

PASTA

Even at its most simple—hard semolina flour and water—pasta is a satisfying and nourishing food. Add eggs and spinach or use wholemeal flour and it becomes a good source of protein, carbohydrates, fibre and minerals. Egg pastas, spinach or green (*verdi*) pastas and wholewheat pastas are sold in fresh and dried form. Flat noodles, assorted shapes, lasagne sheets, tortellini and ravioli are increasingly sold fresh. The most widely available dried pasta varieties are *Spaghetti*; *Tagliatelle* (wide, flat noodles); *Fettuccine* (slightly thinner *tagliatelle*); *Vermicelli* (coils of very thin *spaghetti*); *Macaroni* (long or short cut tubes); *Lasagne* (pasta sheets); *Cannelloni* (large tubes for stuffing); *Tortellini* (twists of stuffed pasta); *Rigatoni* (grooved tubes); *Gemelli* (two short strands coiled together like twins); *Farfalle* or *Cravatte* (bows); *Conchiglie* (shells); *Penne* (macaroni tubes); *Ruote* (wheels); *Fusilli* (twists).

To cook pasta

The method is the same for fresh or dried, but the timing differs according to the shape or thickness, so follow the packet instructions. Allow 50 g (2 oz) dried pasta per head (a little more if using fresh) for a starter. Allow about 125 g (4 oz) fresh or 75 g (3 oz) dried pasta for a main course.

Cook the pasta in plenty of boiling water, ideally allowing about 4 litres (7 pints) per 500 g (1 lb). Add about 1 tablespoon salt and 1 tablespoon oil, which will help stop the water boiling over. Keep the water at a steady, rather than rapid, boil.

The pasta is cooked when it still has a slight bite to it, which the Italians call *al dente*. Fresh pasta takes only about 3 minutes, dried about 12 minutes. Do not overdrain fresh pasta—Italians leave it slightly wet. Rinse it if you wish, in cold water, then toss in a little olive oil or butter and reheat for a few seconds.

NOTES

Ingredients are given in both metric and imperial measures. Use either set of quantities but not a mixture of both in any one recipe.

All spoon measurements are level:
1 tablespoon = one 15 ml spoon
1 teaspoon = one 5 ml spoon.

Ovens should be preheated to the temperature specified.

Freshly ground black pepper is intended where pepper is listed.

Fresh herbs are used unless otherwise stated. If unobtainable, dried herbs can be substituted in cooked dishes but halve the quantities.

Eggs are standard size 3 unless otherwise stated.

Follow basic instructions for cooking rice, pulses and pasta, given in the introduction.

SOUPS & STARTERS

BLACK BEAN AND CHEESE SOUP

2 tablespoons oil
1 leek, sliced
1 clove garlic, crushed
125 g (4 oz) black beans,
    cooked
1.25 litres (2¼ pints)
    vegetable stock
1 tablespoon light brown
    soft sugar
2 sage leaves, chopped
2 slices bread
oil for shallow frying
50 g (2 oz) Cheddar
    cheese, grated
salt and pepper to taste

Serves 4–6
Preparation time:
20 minutes, plus
cooking beans
Cooking time:
25 minutes
Freezing:
Recommended

1. Heat the oil in a large pan, add the leek and garlic and fry until softened. Add the beans, stock, sugar, sage, and plenty of salt and pepper. Bring to the boil, cover and simmer for about 20 minutes.

2. Meanwhile, remove the crusts from the bread and cut into small cubes. Shallow-fry in the hot oil for 1–2 minutes, until golden and crisp. Drain on kitchen paper.

3. Pour the soup into warmed individual bowls and sprinkle the cheese and croûtons on top to serve.

TOMATO AND RICE SOUP

2 tablespoons oil
1 onion, chopped
1 clove garlic, crushed
1 small red pepper, cored,
    seeded and chopped
397 g (14 oz) can chopped
    tomatoes
1 teaspoon chopped
    marjoram
1.25 litres (2¼ pints) stock
1–2 tablespoons
    Worcestershire sauce
2 × 25 g (1 oz) peperami
    sausages, chopped
40 g (1½ oz) long-grain
    rice
salt and pepper to taste
chopped parsley to garnish

Serves 4–6
Preparation time:
10 minutes
Cooking time:
35 minutes
Freezing:
Recommended

1. Heat the oil in a large pan, add the onion, garlic and red pepper and fry gently for about 3 minutes.

2. Add the tomatoes, marjoram, stock, Worcestershire sauce to taste, and salt and pepper. Bring to the boil, cover and simmer for about 15 minutes.

3. Add the peperami and rice, bring back to the boil, cover and simmer for 15 minutes.

4. Pour into warmed individual bowls and sprinkle with parsley to serve.

SUCCOTASH

Succotash is an American-Indian name for a mixture of lima (butter) beans and corn. For a quickly prepared version, use canned beans and frozen corn. This is an ideal soup for vegetarians.

2 fresh sweetcorn cobs or 350 g (12 oz) frozen sweetcorn kernels	*1 thyme sprig, or ¹/₂ teaspoon dried thyme*
25 g (1 oz) butter or margarine	*1 summer savory sprig, or 2 sage leaves*
2 cloves garlic, crushed	*1 teaspoon chopped basil*
1 onion, chopped	*300 ml (¹/₂ pint) milk*
2 celery sticks, sliced	*300 ml (¹/₂ pint) vegetable stock*
125 g (4 oz) butter beans, cooked	*salt and pepper to taste*
	thyme sprigs to garnish

Serves 4
Preparation time: 5 minutes, plus cooking beans
Cooking time: 15 minutes
Freezing: Recommended

1. If using fresh sweetcorn, stand the cobs upright and using a sharp knife strip the kernels by cutting downwards.
2. Melt the butter or margarine in a pan, add the garlic, onion and celery and sauté gently for about 5 minutes, until softened.
3. Add the remaining ingredients, and season well with salt and pepper. Bring to the boil, then cover and simmer for 10 minutes.
4. Check seasoning and serve garnished with thyme.

DOLMADES

150 ml (¹/₄ pint) olive oil	*150 ml (¹/₄ pint) water*
250 g (8 oz) onions, chopped	*1 tablespoon pine nuts*
125 g (4 oz) long-grain rice	*1 teaspoon salt*
40 g (1¹/₂ oz) currants	*pepper to taste*
1 tablespoon chopped dill	*227 g (8 oz) pack vine leaves in brine*
1 tablespoon chopped mint (optional)	*juice of ¹/₂ lemon*
	lemon wedges to garnish

1. Heat half of the oil in a large pan, add the onion and fry gently until softened. Add the rice, cover and cook gently for 5 minutes.
2. Add the currants, herbs, water, nuts, and salt and pepper. Bring to the boil, then cover and simmer gently for 5 minutes.

3. Meanwhile, drain and rinse the vine leaves carefully. Lay them out on a clean worktop, rib side upwards with the stalk pointing towards you.

4. Put 1 teaspoon of the rice mixture at the stalk end of each leaf. Fold the bottom edge up, then fold the sides in and roll up firmly, but not too tightly.

5. Place side by side in a large shallow pan with a lid. Pour over the remaining oil, the lemon juice and enough water just to cover the top of the rolls.

6. Place an old heatproof china or glass plate on top of the rolls to hold them down, bring to the boil, then cover and simmer for 1 hour. Leave to cool in the pan, then remove carefully and arrange on a serving dish.

7. Serve chilled, garnished with lemon wedges.

Serves 4–6
(Makes about 30)
Preparation time:
45 minutes
Cooking time:
1 hour
Freezing:
Not recommended

BEANS À LA GRECQUE

Use any white bean for this recipe, although the white kidney or haricot beans look the nicest. Overnight chilling allows the flavours to mature.

300 ml (¹/₂ pint) water
2 tablespoons tomato
  purée
2 tablespoons olive or
  sunflower oil
2 tablespoons vinegar
1 clove garlic, crushed
¹/₂ teaspoon ground
  coriander
1 small onion, chopped

1 large courgette, sliced
125 g (4 oz) button
  mushrooms, halved
125 g (4 oz) white beans,
  cooked
3 tablespoons chopped
  parsley
salt and pepper to taste
chopped parsley to serve

Serves 4
Preparation time:
10 minutes, plus
cooking beans and
chilling
Cooking time:
8–10 minutes
Freezing:
Recommended

1. Place the water, tomato purée, oil, vinegar, garlic, coriander, and salt and pepper in a large saucepan, bring to the boil, then simmer for about 5 minutes.
2. Add the onion, courgette and mushrooms and cook for 3–5 minutes, until just cooked but still quite crunchy. Stir in the beans and parsley and check the seasoning. Leave to cool, then chill overnight.
3. Sprinkle with parsley and serve with French bread.

FALAFELS WITH TAHINI CREAM

Falafels are little protein-packed patties eaten as street food in the Middle East, tucked into pittas with salad and served with tahini cream. The cream will keep for up to 7 days in a screw-topped jar in the refrigerator.

125 g (4 oz) chick peas,
  cooked
1 clove garlic, crushed
2 tablespoons chopped
  parsley
2 tablespoons chopped
  coriander, or
  ¹/₂ teaspoon ground
¹/₂ teaspoon ground
  cumin
1 tablespoon wholemeal
  flour
1 teaspoon salt

pepper to taste
oil for shallow frying
FOR THE TAHINI CREAM:
6 tablespoons tahini (see
  page 17)
150 ml (¹/₄ pint) water
juice of ¹/₂ lemon
1 clove garlic, crushed
TO SERVE:
4 pitta breads, halved
2 tomatoes, sliced
few lettuce leaves
cucumber slices

1. Drain the chick peas. Place in a blender or food processor and work until smooth but thick. Add the remaining ingredients and work until well blended.

2. With wet hands, divide the mixture into 8 pieces and shape into flat patties. Shallow-fry in hot oil for about 6 minutes, turning once, until golden. Drain on kitchen paper.

3. To make the tahini cream, gradually mix the tahini and water together until smooth. Stir in the lemon juice, garlic, and salt and pepper to taste.

4. To serve, place a falafel in each pitta, with a portion of the salad ingredients and a spoonful of tahini cream. Serve hot or cold.

Makes 8
Preparation time:
15 minutes, plus
cooking chick peas
Cooking time:
6 minutes
Freezing:
Not recommended

PEA, TOFU AND AVOCADO DIP

Most pulses are good bases for creamy, low-fat dips. This one uses dried green peas, with added flavouring and creaminess from the avocado and tofu.

*125 g (4 oz) dried green
  peas, cooked
75 g (3 oz) tofu bean curd
1/2 ripe avocado, peeled
1 clove garlic, crushed
2 spring onions, chopped
1 tablespoon chopped
  parsley*

*1/2 teaspoon ground
  cumin
1 teaspoon Worcestershire
  sauce
juice of 1/2 lemon
salt and pepper to taste*

**Makes 300 ml
(1/2 pint)
Preparation time:**
10 minutes, plus
cooking peas
Freezing:
Recommended

1. Place all the ingredients in a blender or food processor and work until smooth. Chill until required.
2. Serve with crackers, tortilla chips or raw vegetables.

VARIATION

Add a little chilli powder or hot pepper sauce, and chopped green pepper, chopped tomato and stuffed olives.

RED BEAN CHILLI DIP

A spicy Mexican-style dip. Use mild or hot chilli powder according to taste.

*2 tablespoons oil
1 small onion, chopped
1 clove garlic, crushed
1 teaspoon chilli powder
1 teaspoon ground cumin
1 tablespoon tomato purée
1 tablespoon red wine
  vinegar*

*125 g (4 oz) red kidney or
  pinto beans, cooked for
  1 1/2 hours
113 g (4 oz) carton cream
  cheese or curd cheese
50 g (2 oz) matured
  Cheddar cheese, grated
salt and pepper to taste*

**Makes about
450 ml (3/4 pint)
Preparation time:**
10 minutes, plus
cooking beans
Cooking time:
5 minutes
Freezing:
Recommended

1. Heat the oil in a small pan, add the onion and garlic and fry gently for about 4 minutes. Add the spices and fry for 1 minute, then stir in the tomato purée and vinegar. Leave to cool.
2. Place the beans, cheeses and onion mixture in a blender or food processor and work until the consistency of thick mayonnaise; add a little water if necessary. Check the seasoning. Chill until required.
3. Serve with raw vegetables or tortilla chips.

HUMMUS

This will keep in the refrigerator for about 3 days. Tahini is a paste made from ground sesame seeds, sold in jars.

*100 g (3½ oz) chick peas,
    cooked for 1½ hours
4 tablespoons tahini
3 tablespoons lemon juice
1 clove garlic, crushed*

*salt and pepper to taste
TO GARNISH:
cayenne pepper
chopped parsley
olive oil (optional)*

1. Place all the ingredients in a blender or food processor and work together until smooth and creamy, adding a little water if necessary; hummus should have a soft spooning consistency, not too dry.

2. Check the seasoning, then spoon into a serving bowl. Sprinkle with a little cayenne and parsley and trickle over a little olive oil, if you wish. Serve as a dip with vegetable crudités or pieces of pitta bread, or use as a sauce with kebabs, burgers or chops.

**Makes about
300 ml (½ pint)
Preparation time:**
5 minutes, plus
cooking chick peas
Freezing:
Recommended

QUICK DISHES

TAGLIATELLE WITH PESTO

Use only fresh basil, fresh Parmesan and the best olive oil you can afford, for this superb pasta sauce.

fresh basil leaves to fill a 300 ml (½ pint) mug
50 g (2 oz) pine nuts
125 g (4 oz) Parmesan cheese, grated
2 cloves garlic, crushed
6 tablespoons olive oil
500 g (1 lb) fresh green and white tagliatelle
knob of butter
salt and pepper to taste
basil leaves to garnish

Serves 4, or 6 as a starter
Preparation time: 10 minutes
Cooking time: 3–5 minutes
Freezing: Not recommended

1. First make the sauce, either by pounding with a pestle and mortar, or in a blender or food processor: work the basil, pine nuts, cheese, garlic and plenty of pepper together until well mixed. Slowly add the oil, blending or pounding until incorporated. Set aside.
2. Cook the pasta, drain and toss in the butter. Mix in the pesto. Serve immediately, garnished with basil.

SPAGHETTI ALLA CARBONARA

This dish must be eaten freshly cooked; it will not reheat. The heat of the pasta is sufficient to set the eggs lightly.

350 g (12 oz) dried spaghetti
2 tablespoons olive oil
1 clove garlic, crushed
1 small onion, chopped
125 g (4 oz) smoked back bacon, derinded and chopped
3 eggs, beaten
4 tablespoons single cream
50–75 g (2–3 oz) Parmesan cheese, grated
2 tablespoons chopped parsley
grated nutmeg, salt and pepper to taste

Serves 4, or 6 as a starter
Preparation time: 10 minutes
Cooking time: About 12 minutes
Freezing: Not recommended

1. Cook the pasta, then drain.
2. Meanwhile heat the oil in a pan, add the garlic, onion and bacon and fry until softened. Toss into the hot pasta and season with nutmeg, salt and pepper.
3. Beat the eggs with the cream and half of the cheese. Season with pepper. Pour onto the pasta, stirring.
4. Transfer to warmed serving plates and sprinkle with the parsley. Serve the remaining cheese separately.

RISI E BISI

This deliciously simple Venetian risotto-soup makes an ideal light lunch.

50 g (2 oz) butter
1 onion, chopped
3 rashers streaky bacon,
    derinded and chopped
250 g (8 oz) Italian risotto
    rice
1.25 litres (2¼ pints)
    chicken stock

½ chicken stock cube
pinch of sugar
500 g (1 lb) frozen peas
50 g (2 oz) Parmesan
    cheese, grated
2 tablespoons chopped
    parsley
salt and pepper to taste

Serves 4
Preparation time:
10 minutes
Cooking time:
20 minutes
Freezing:
Not recommended

1. Melt half of the butter in a pan, add the onion and bacon and sauté for about 5 minutes, until softened. Add the rice and fry for 1 minute.
2. Pour in the stock, add the stock cube half, sugar, salt and pepper. Bring to the boil, stir, then cover and simmer for about 12 minutes.
3. Add the peas and cook for 3 minutes.
4. Stir in the remaining butter, the Parmesan cheese and parsley. The mixture should be like a very thick soup; add a little extra stock or water if it is too dry.
5. Serve in individual warmed bowls with crusty bread and salad.

SPICED RICE WITH PRAWNS

A quick, spicy supper or light lunch dish. For best results, use Basmati rice.

2 tablespoons oil
1 onion, chopped
1 clove garlic, crushed
1 cm (½ inch) piece fresh
    root ginger, grated
250 g (8 oz) long-grain
    rice
1 teaspoon mild curry
    powder
25 g (1 oz) creamed
    coconut, in pieces
600 ml (1 pint) chicken
    stock

250 g (8 oz) peeled prawns
2 tablespoons chopped
    coriander leaves
4 tablespoons natural
    yogurt (optional)
25 g (1 oz) flaked
    almonds, toasted
salt and pepper to taste
lemon slices and
    coriander leaves to
    garnish

1. Heat the oil in a large pan, add the onion, garlic and ginger and fry for about 5 minutes.

2. Add the rice and fry for about 2 minutes, until opaque, then sprinkle in the curry powder and fry for 1 minute. Add the creamed coconut, stirring until dissolved.

3. Add the stock, and salt and pepper. Bring to the boil, cover and simmer for about 15 minutes, until the rice is tender and the liquid absorbed.

4. Stir in the prawns and coriander and heat well. If using, stir in the yogurt. Sprinkle with the almonds and garnish with lemon and coriander to serve.

Serves 4
Preparation time:
10 minutes
Cooking time:
25 minutes
Freezing:
Not recommended

FRIJOLES REFRITOS

Refried beans or *frijoles refritos* are something of a staple food in Mexico, served in many ways. The idea behind frying already-cooked beans is to further develop their flavour. This is the authentic method of refrying, using the bean cooking liquor; however you can substitute water. If you have any left over—no problem, simply refry them again. The flavour gets better still!

3–4 tablespoons oil
1 small onion, chopped
250 g (8 oz) red kidney,
*   pinto or black beans,*
*   cooked until very soft*

about 450 ml (¾ pint)
*   cooking liquor from*
*   beans*
salt and pepper to taste

Serves 4
Preparation time:
5 minutes, plus
cooking beans
Cooking time:
10–15 minutes
Freezing:
Recommended

1. Heat the oil in a large frying pan, add the onion and fry gently.
2. Add about a quarter of the beans and a little of the cooking liquor, mashing with a potato masher, and stirring occasionally as they cook. Gradually add the remaining beans and cooking liquor, mashing and stirring until you have a coarse purée. Season with salt and pepper.
3. When the purée has started to dry around the edge, it is ready. Serve with tomato coulis (see below) or the spicy tomato sauce on page 36 if you wish.

USES FOR REFRIED BEANS

1. Serve on fried tortillas or tostadas, topped with a fried egg or tomato coulis and slices of avocado or grated cheese.
2. Mix with rice as a quick stuffing for green peppers or tomatoes and top with grated cheese.
3. Spoon onto pancakes, roll up, spoon over tomato coulis, sprinkle with grated cheese and reheat in the oven.
4. Mix with cream cheese, grated cheese and tomato purée for a quick dip.
5. Serve on toast or a hot crispy roll, topped with an egg or melted Cheddar cheese and crumbled grilled bacon.
6. Use as a filling for Enchilladas (page 36).

TOMATO COULIS

Place 500 g (1 lb) chopped ripe tomatoes, ½ teaspoon sugar, 1 teaspoon salt, ½ teaspoon dried mixed herbs, 2 tablespoons French dressing and pepper to taste in a saucepan. Cover and simmer for 10 minutes, then rub through a sieve. A delicious fresh tomato sauce to serve with refried beans.

LENTILS WITH SPICY SAUSAGE

Lentils make wonderful quick stews, especially when mixed with cured and smoked meats or sausages. This stew will go nicely with crusty bread or potatoes, or it can be served as a sauce for spaghetti.

50 g (2 oz) smoked or sweetcure bacon, derinded and chopped
1 onion, chopped
1 clove garlic, crushed
250 g (8 oz) lentils
397 g (14 oz) can tomatoes

250 g (8 oz) cured and cooked sausage, e.g. chorizo or Polish cabanos
750 ml (1¼ pints) water
1 teaspoon paprika
salt and pepper to taste

Serves 4
Preparation time: 10 minutes
Cooking time: 25–45 minutes, depending on lentils used
Freezing: Recommended

1. Fry the bacon in a large pan until the fat runs, add the onion and garlic and sauté until softened.
2. Add the remaining ingredients, bring to the boil, cover and simmer for 20–25 minutes if using red lentils, 35–40 minutes if using green or brown. Serve hot.

PORK FRIED RICE IN LETTUCE

Light, tasty and colourful, these make a lovely quick lunch dish or starter. An ideal recipe for using leftover rice—you will need 200 g (7 oz) cooked weight.

4 large crisp curly lettuce leaves
2–3 tablespoons sunflower oil
2 eggs, beaten
6–8 tablespoons chicken stock
2 tablespoons soy sauce
1 tablespoon dry sherry
1 tablespoon cornflour
2 teaspoons sesame oil (optional)

125 g (4 oz) minced pork
1 clove garlic, crushed
2.5 cm (1 inch) piece fresh root ginger, grated
4 spring onions, sliced
125 g (4 oz) bean sprouts
125 g (4 oz) long-grain rice, cooked
4 teaspoons hoisin or barbecue sauce
salt and pepper to taste

Serves 2, or 4 as a starter
Preparation time: 10 minutes
Cooking time: 10 minutes
Freezing: Not recommended

1. Place the lettuce leaves on a large platter or individual plates.
2. Heat 1 tablespoon of the oil in a small saucepan, add the eggs, and salt and pepper and cook, stirring only occasionally, until they are scrambled firm but not overcooked. Immediately transfer to a bowl.
3. Place the stock, soy sauce, sherry, cornflour and sesame oil, if using, in a cup and stir until smooth.
4. Heat the remaining oil in a wok or large frying pan, add the pork, garlic and ginger and stir-fry for 2–3 minutes, until browned.
5. Add the spring onions and bean sprouts and stir-fry for 1 minute.
6. Stir in the stock mixture, season with salt and pepper, then add the rice and heat through.
7. Spoon into the centre of each lettuce leaf, then top with the egg. Trickle a teaspoon of hoisin or barbecue sauce over each serving.
8. To eat, fold over the lettuce leaves like envelopes and eat with fingers.

VARIATION

This is an ideal recipe for using up leftover cooked and minced chicken or spicy sausage. Omit the pork. Stir-fry the ginger, garlic, spring onions and bean sprouts as above. Stir in the stock mixture and seasoning. Add the chicken or spicy sausage, with the rice, and heat through.

PASTA WITH MUSSELS AND PRAWNS

*250 g (8 oz) dried pasta
shapes
2 tablespoons olive oil
1 red or green chilli,
seeded and sliced
1 clove garlic, crushed
227 g (8 oz) can mussels
in brine
150 ml (¼ pint) dry white
wine or cider*

*397 g (14 oz) can chopped
tomatoes
1 tablespoon chopped
marjoram or 1 teaspoon
dried
125 g (4 oz) peeled prawns
salt and pepper to taste
chopped parsley to garnish*

Serves 4
Preparation time:
10 minutes
Cooking time:
About 12 minutes
Freezing:
Not recommended

1. Cook the pasta.
2. Meanwhile, heat the oil in a pan, add the chilli and garlic and sauté gently. Strain the liquor from the mussels into the pan, then add the wine or cider. Simmer for about 5 minutes, until reduced by half.
3. Add the tomatoes and marjoram and cook for about 3 minutes, then add the mussels and prawns. Cook for about 2 minutes, until thoroughly heated. Season with salt and pepper.
4. Drain the pasta, add to the sauce and toss well. Serve immediately, sprinkled with parsley.

CHICKEN LIVER PAN PASTA

*200 g (7 oz) dried pasta
 shapes*
25 g (1 oz) butter
*250 g (8 oz) frozen
 chicken livers, thawed
 and sliced thinly*
*50 g (2 oz) bacon,
 derinded and chopped*
2 courgettes, sliced
2 leeks, sliced

*125 g (4 oz) button
 mushrooms, sliced*
*150 ml (¼ pint) dry cider
 or stock*
*2 tablespoons dry
 vermouth*
½ teaspoon dried sage
*4 tablespoons natural
 yogurt or single cream*
salt and pepper to taste

1. Cook the pasta.
2. Meanwhile, melt the butter in a pan, add the liver and bacon and fry for 2 minutes. Add the courgettes, leeks and mushrooms and stir-fry for 5 minutes.
3. Add the cider or stock, vermouth, sage, and salt and pepper. Cover and simmer for 5 minutes.
4. Drain the pasta, add to the sauce with the yogurt or cream and toss gently. Serve immediately.

Serves 4
Preparation time:
10 minutes
Cooking time:
About 12 minutes
Freezing:
Not recommended

VARIATION
Use lambs' or calves' liver in place of the chicken livers.
Add carrots or red pepper strips for colour.

PASTA IN GREEN GARLIC SAUCE

A quick supper dish for those who enjoy soft garlic cheese—and have never thought of cooking with it before! It makes a particularly good pasta sauce, especially suitable for vegetarians.

25 g (1 oz) butter
1 small onion, sliced
250 g (8 oz) button
mushrooms, sliced
500 g (1 lb) fresh tagliatelle
or other ribbon pasta
1 tablespoon olive oil
250 g (8 oz) frozen leaf
spinach, thawed

2 × 62.5 g (2.2 oz) packets
full-fat soft cheese with
garlic and herbs, or
113 g (4 oz) carton
low-fat version
300 ml (½ pint) milk
grated nutmeg, salt and
pepper to taste
chopped parsley to serve
(optional)

Serves 4
Preparation time:
10 minutes
Cooking time:
About 12 minutes
Freezing:
Not recommended

1. Melt the butter in a pan, add the onion and fry gently for about 3 minutes. Add the mushrooms, cover and simmer for 5 minutes.
2. Cook the pasta, drain and toss in the oil with a little nutmeg.
3. Meanwhile, chop the spinach, then add to the mushroom mixture and heat through for 1–2 minutes.
4. Add the cheese and allow to melt slightly, then stir in the milk; if you use low-fat cheese, you may not need to add all the milk as the cheese is not as thick. Season well with salt and pepper.
5. Toss in the pasta and mix well. Serve on individual warmed plates, sprinkled with parsley if you wish.

TUNA AND NOODLE BAKE

250 g (8 oz) dried
tagliatelle
3 carrots, chopped
3 leeks, sliced
2 celery sticks, sliced
125 g (4 oz) mushrooms,
sliced
300 ml (½ pint) water
40 g (1½ oz) butter
200 g (7 oz) can tuna,
drained and flaked

2 tablespoons wholemeal
flour
300 ml (½ pint) milk
¼ teaspoon grated
nutmeg
1 teaspoon dried mixed
herbs
125 g (4 oz) matured
Cheddar cheese, grated
3 tablespoons fresh
breadcrumbs
salt and pepper to taste

1. Cook the pasta.
2. Meanwhile, place the vegetables and water in a saucepan, add 15 g (½ oz) of the butter, and salt and pepper. Cover, bring to the boil, then simmer for about 5 minutes, until just tender. Drain, reserving the liquor.
3. Drain the pasta and mix with the tuna and vegetables.
4. Place the remaining butter in a saucepan with the flour, milk and reserved vegetable water. Bring slowly to the boil, stirring constantly with a whisk. Add the nutmeg, herbs, salt and pepper, and simmer for about 5 minutes.
5. Stir in all but 2 tablespoons of the cheese. Stir the sauce into the pasta, then spoon into a gratin dish.
6. Mix the remaining cheese with the breadcrumbs and sprinkle over the top. Place under a preheated hot grill until browned. Serve immediately, on its own.

Serves 4
Preparation time:
20 minutes
Cooking time:
About 12 minutes
Freezing:
Recommended

MAIN COURSE DISHES

PAELLA DE MONTANA

pinch of saffron threads
3 tablespoons olive oil
4 rabbit portions
4 chicken portions
250 g (8 oz) pork fillet,
  sliced
2 cloves garlic, crushed
397 g (14 oz) can chopped
  tomatoes

6 tablespoons chopped
  parsley
250 g (8 oz) long-grain
  rice
400 ml (14 fl oz) water
175 ml (6 fl oz) dry white
  wine
salt and pepper to taste

Serves 4–6
Preparation time:
10 minutes
Cooking time:
35 minutes
Freezing:
Recommended

1. Soak the saffron in 1 tablespoon warm water.
2. Heat the oil in a large pan, add the meats and fry for
10 minutes, until well browned. Remove and set aside.
3. Add the garlic, tomatoes, saffron with its water, 4 tablespoons of the parsley, and salt and pepper. Cook for about
10 minutes, until thick.
4. Add the rice, water, wine and meats. Bring to the boil,
then simmer for about 15 minutes, shaking the pan occasionally. Sprinkle with the remaining parsley to serve.

SQUID PROVENÇALE

250 g (8 oz) long-grain
  rice
2 tablespoons olive oil
1 onion, sliced
2 cloves garlic, crushed
1 green pepper, cored,
  seeded and sliced
150 ml (¼ pint) dry white
  wine

397 g (14 oz) can chopped
  tomatoes
4 tablespoons water
1 small rosemary sprig
500 g (1 lb) cleaned squid,
  sliced
2 tablespoons brandy
salt and pepper to taste
rosemary sprigs to garnish

Serves 4
Preparation time:
15 minutes
Cooking time:
15 minutes
Freezing:
Not recommended

1. Cook the rice.
2. Meanwhile, heat the oil in a pan, add the onion, garlic
and green pepper and fry until softened. Add the wine and
cook until reduced by half.
3. Add the remaining ingredients, except the brandy, and
simmer for 10 minutes, stirring. Stir in the brandy and
cook for another minute.
4. Garnish with rosemary and serve with the rice.

BEANS 'N RICE

Hoppin' John, Limpin' Susan, Moors and Christians—whatever the name, the combination of beans and rice appears in many American and West Indian cuisines. The beans can be black, red or white. The dish may be hot and spicy or mild—adapt it to your own taste.

1 tablespoon oil
250 g (8 oz) minced pork
1 onion, chopped
1 green chilli, seeded and chopped finely
350 g (12 oz) long-grain rice
1 beef tomato, skinned and sliced

900 ml (1½ pints) stock
1 thyme sprig
125 g (4 oz) beans (see above), cooked
50 g (2 oz) creamed coconut
2 tablespoons chopped parsley or coriander
salt and pepper to taste

Serves 4
Preparation time:
10 minutes, plus cooking beans
Cooking time:
About 25 minutes
Freezing:
Recommended

1. Heat the oil in a pan, add the pork and onion and fry for about 5 minutes. Add the chilli and rice and fry for about 2 minutes, until the rice turns opaque.
2. Add the tomato, stock, thyme, and salt and pepper, bring to the boil, cover and simmer for 10 minutes.
3. Add the beans and a little extra stock or water if the mixture looks dry. Cover and cook for 5 minutes, until the stock is absorbed and the rice just tender. Gradually stir in the creamed coconut until it has melted, then stir in the parsley or coriander. Serve hot.

CARIBBEAN PORK AND RICE

250 g (8 oz) diced pork
75 g (3 oz) salt pork or ham, diced
50 g (2 oz) bacon, derinded and diced
1 onion, sliced
1 large chilli, seeded and sliced
1 green pepper, cored, seeded and sliced
2 bay leaves
juice of 2 limes
1 teaspoon ground allspice
½ teaspoon ground cinnamon

2 tablespoons oil
350 g (12 oz) long-grain rice
397 g (14 oz) can chopped tomatoes
900 ml (1½ pints) stock
125 g (4 oz) kidney or pinto beans, cooked
2 tablespoons capers (optional)
salt and pepper to taste
TO GARNISH:
1 avocado
6–8 radishes, sliced
coriander sprigs

1. Place the meats, onion, chilli, green pepper, bay leaves, lime juice, spices, and salt and pepper in a bowl, cover and chill overnight.

2. Heat the oil in a pan, add the marinated ingredients and marinade and fry for 5 minutes, stirring occasionally.

3. Add the rice and fry for about 2 minutes, then add the tomatoes, stock, and salt and pepper. Bring to the boil, cover and simmer for 15 minutes.

4. Add the beans and capers, if using, and cook for 5 minutes. Remove the bay leaves and transfer to warmed individual serving plates.

5. Peel and slice the avocado and arrange around the edge of the plates with the radishes and coriander.

Serves 4–6
Preparation time:
20 minutes, plus
cooking beans and
marinating
Cooking time:
25–30 minutes
Freezing:
Recommended

LAMB STEAKS WITH BEANS

2 tablespoons olive oil
4 chump chops
1 rosemary sprig or ½
teaspoon dried
2 cloves garlic, crushed
125 g (4 oz) haricot,
cannellini or flageolet
beans, cooked

125 g (4 oz) baby onions
4 tablespoons dry white
wine or cider
300 ml (½ pint) stock
knob of butter
salt and pepper to taste
chopped parsley to garnish

Serves 4
Preparation time:
5 minutes, plus
cooking beans
Cooking time:
25 minutes
Freezing:
Recommended

1. Heat the oil in a frying pan, add the lamb and cook for
3–5 minutes on each side, according to taste. Season with
salt and pepper while cooking and sprinkle with the
rosemary. Remove and keep warm.
2. Add the garlic, beans and onions to the pan and cook
for about 5 minutes.
3. Pour in the wine or cider and cook until reduced a little,
then stir in the stock. Season with salt and pepper and
simmer for about 10 minutes, then stir in the butter.
4. Sprinkle with parsley and serve with crusty bread and
salad.

HADDOCK AND BEAN CASSOULET

Cassoulets are usually mixed meat and bean stews, but this
one uses firm fish with beans for a lighter, quicker meal.

750 g (1½ lb) Finnan
haddock
250 g (8 oz) monkfish tail
1 litre (1¾ pints) fish stock
or water
1 large bay leaf
25 g (1 oz) butter
1 onion, chopped
1 celery stick, sliced
1 carrot, chopped
1 clove garlic, crushed
50 g (2 oz) sweetcure
bacon, derinded and
chopped
125 g (4 oz) salt pork or
ham
4 tablespoons dry white
wine or cider

175 g (6 oz) haricot beans,
cooked
½ teaspoon ground mace
1 each thyme, rosemary
and savory sprig, or
½ teaspoon each dried
herb
pinch of saffron threads,
soaked in 1 tablespoon
warm water (optional)
4 tomatoes, skinned and
quartered
salt and pepper to taste
FOR THE TOPPING:
3 tablespoons fresh
breadcrumbs
2 tablespoons chopped
parsley

1. Place the fish, stock or water, bay leaf and black pepper in a saucepan and cook gently for 10–15 minutes, until the flesh just flakes. Drain, reserving about 600 ml (1 pint) of the liquor.

2. Skin, bone and flake the fish and set aside.

3. Melt the butter in a pan, add the onion, celery, carrot and garlic and sauté for about 5 minutes. Add the bacon and salt pork or ham and cook for 3 minutes.

4. Pour in the reserved fish liquor and wine or cider. Add the beans, mace and herbs and cook for about 10 minutes, until the liquid has nearly all been reduced.

5. Add the saffron and its water, if using, fish and tomatoes. Check the seasoning, then transfer to a shallow casserole.

6. Mix the breadcrumbs and parsley together and sprinkle over the top. Bake in a preheated oven, 190°C/375°F/Gas Mark 5, for 30–35 minutes, until the top is crisp and golden. Serve hot.

Serves 4
Preparation time:
50 minutes, plus cooking beans
Cooking time:
30–35 minutes
Freezing:
Recommended, if using fresh fish

ENCHILLADAS

Meaning literally 'filled with chilli', enchilladas are fried tortillas dipped in a spicy sauce, rolled around a filling and then baked. You could use refried beans (see page 22) as a filling, or try this quick creamy bean filling.

2 tablespoons oil
1 onion, chopped
1 clove garlic, crushed
213 g (7¹/₂ oz) can red kidney, borlotti or cannellini beans, or a mixture, drained
25 g (1 oz) peperami sausage, chopped
142 ml (5 fl oz) carton soured cream
125 g (4 oz) Cheddar cheese, grated
oil for shallow frying
12 canned tortillas

FOR THE SAUCE:
397 g (14 oz) can tomatoes
113 g (3.99 oz) can green chillies in brine, drained
2 spring onions, chopped
3 tablespoons each chopped coriander and parsley
¹/₂ teaspoon sugar
salt and pepper to taste
TO GARNISH:
coriander or flat-leaved parsley

Serves 4
Preparation time:
25 minutes
Cooking time:
25 minutes
Freezing:
Not recommended

1. Heat the oil in a pan, add the onion and garlic and fry for 5 minutes. Add the beans, mashing slightly, and fry for 5 minutes, stirring occasionally. Add the peperami, soured cream and three quarters of the cheese. Season well with salt and pepper.
2. To make the sauce, place all the ingredients in a blender or food processor and work until smooth.
3. Heat a little oil in a small frying pan and fry one tortilla at a time for about 5 seconds on each side; drain.
4. Dip the tortillas in the sauce briefly until just softened, spoon a little filling on one side and roll up.
5. Place in a shallow ovenproof dish, trickling over a little sauce as you stack them. Spoon the remaining sauce over the top.
6. Sprinkle with the remaining cheese and bake in a preheated oven, 190°C/375°F/Gas Mark 5, for about 25 minutes, until the cheese is bubbling. Serve immediately, garnished with coriander or parsley.

CHILLI CON CARNE

This dish is best made the day before it is eaten.

2 tablespoons oil
500 g (1 lb) stewing beef,
    diced
1 onion, chopped
1–2 green chillies, chopped
2 cloves garlic, crushed
1 tablespoon paprika
1–2 teaspoons chilli
    powder
1 tablespoon ground
    cumin

2 tablespoons tomato
    purée
600 ml (1 pint) beef stock
    or water
2 teaspoons dried oregano
2 bay leaves
125 g (4 oz) red kidney or
    pinto beans, soaked
    overnight
salt and pepper to taste

Serves 4
Preparation time:
15 minutes, plus
soaking beans
Cooking time:
2 hours
Freezing:
Recommended

1. Heat the oil in a large pan, add the beef and fry, stirring, for about 5 minutes until browned. Set aside.
2. Add the onion, chilli and garlic to the pan, and sauté for about 3 minutes, then add the spices and fry for 1 minute.
3. Add the tomato purée, stock or water, oregano, bay leaves, and salt and pepper, return the meat, cover and simmer for 1 hour.
4. Meanwhile, drain the beans and cook rapidly in boiling water for 10 minutes; drain. Add them to the chilli mixture and cook for a further hour, or until the beans are tender.
5. Serve with plain boiled rice.

PIGEON AND CHICK PEA CASSEROLE

3 tablespoons plain flour
1 teaspoon chilli powder
1/2 teaspoon salt
4 wood pigeons
2 tablespoons olive oil
75 g (3 oz) streaky bacon,
    derinded and diced
2 carrots, sliced
1 litre (1 3/4 pints) chicken
    stock
1 onion, studded with 8
    cloves

2 bay leaves
2 tablespoons tomato
    purée
125 g (4 oz) long-grain
    rice
1/4 small white cabbage,
    shredded
125 g (4 oz) chorizo
    sausage, chopped
125 g (4 oz) chick peas,
    cooked
pepper to taste

1. Mix the flour, chilli, salt, and pepper to taste in a polythene bag, then toss the pigeons in it. Reserve any leftover seasoned flour.

2. Heat the oil in a pan, add the pigeons and brown well. Remove from the pan and set aside. Add the bacon to the pan and fry for about 2 minutes, then add the carrots and fry lightly for 5 minutes. Transfer to a large casserole and place the pigeons on top.

3. Sprinkle the seasoned flour into the pan and stir well. Pour in the stock and bring to the boil, stirring. Pour over the pigeons. Add the onion, bay leaves and tomato purée. Cover and cook in a preheated oven, 180°C/350°F/Gas Mark 4, for 30 minutes.

4. Add the rice, cabbage, sausage and chick peas, cover and return to the oven for 30 minutes. Serve immediately.

Serves 4
Preparation time: 30 minutes, plus cooking chick peas
Cooking time: 1 hour
Freezing: Recommended if using fresh pigeons

COUS COUS WITH SPICED LAMB

500 g (1 lb) cous cous
25 g (1 oz) butter
500 g (1 lb) boned
shoulder of lamb, diced
2 onions, quartered
2 carrots, sliced
2.5 cm (1 inch) piece fresh
root ginger
1/2 teaspoon turmeric
1/2 teaspoon ground
cinnamon
1 teaspoon ground
coriander
1 litre (1¾ pints) stock
1 small bulb fennel,
quartered
230 g (8 oz) can tomatoes
75 g (3 oz) raisins
juice of 1 lemon
125 g (4 oz) chick peas,
cooked
salt and pepper to taste

Serves 4–6
Preparation time:
20 minutes, plus
cooking chick peas
Cooking time:
About 35 minutes
Freezing:
Recommended

1. Place the cous cous in a bowl, cover with hot water and drain. Spread out on a clean tray and leave for about 20 minutes; sprinkle with a little water about every 5 minutes and work the grains with your hands to free them of any lumps.
2. Meanwhile, melt the butter in a pan, add the lamb and fry until well browned. Add the onions, carrots and ginger and fry for about 5 minutes, until softened.
3. Sprinkle in the spices and fry for 1 minute, then stir in the remaining ingredients and bring to the boil.
4. Put the cous cous into a steamer and place on top of the stew. When the steam starts to rise, cover and simmer for about 30 minutes.
5. Serve the cous cous topped with the spiced lamb.

CHILLI AND CHICKEN TORTILLAS

Ready-made tortillas are now quite easy to buy in cans. Usually they are fried, filled and folded into *tacos*, but I also like to mould them while hot into little baskets and fill them with a spicy filling.

2 tablespoons oil
1 onion, chopped
230 g (8 oz) can tomatoes
2 tablespoons tomato
purée
1/2 × 113 g (3.99 oz) can
green chillies in brine,
drained and chopped
432 g (15¼ oz) can
borlotti beans, drained
125 g (4 oz) cooked
chicken, diced
12 stuffed green olives,
sliced
oil for shallow frying
8 canned tortillas
salt and pepper to taste
TO GARNISH:
shredded lettuce
1 ripe avocado, sliced

1. Heat the oil in a pan, add the onion and fry for 5 minutes. Add the tomatoes with their juice, tomato purée and chillies and simmer for 5 minutes or until most of the liquid has reduced. Stir in the beans, chicken and olives and cook for 2 minutes. Season well with salt and pepper.

2. Heat a little oil in a small frying pan and fry the tortillas one at a time for about 5 seconds on each side. Remove with tongs and immediately press over an upturned ramekin dish covered with kitchen paper. Press into shape, then carefully remove and place upside down on a wire rack to drain.

3. Place shredded lettuce in the tortilla baskets, fill with the bean mixture and garnish with the avocado slices.

Serves 4, or 8 as a snack
Preparation time: 20 minutes
Cooking time: 15 minutes
Freezing: Not recommended

RAGÙ ALLA BOLOGNESE

The most famous spaghetti sauce which, when cooked authentically, is a far cry from the usual mince cooked with a can of tomatoes. Serve it with any pasta or use in lasagne or cannelloni.

2 tablespoons olive oil
25 g (1 oz) butter
250 g (8 oz) minced beef
125 g (4 oz) chicken livers, chopped
125 g (4 oz) unsmoked bacon, derinded and chopped finely
1 onion, chopped
2 cloves garlic, crushed
1 carrot, chopped
1 celery stick, chopped
150 ml (¼ pint) dry white wine

300 ml (½ pint) beef stock
4–6 tablespoons tomato purée
1 bay leaf
grated nutmeg, salt and pepper to taste
TO SERVE:
350 g (12 oz) dried spaghetti or tagliatelle
a little olive oil
50 g (2 oz) Parmesan cheese, grated

Serves 4
Preparation time:
25 minutes
Cooking time:
25–30 minutes
Freezing:
Recommended for sauce only

1. Heat the oil and butter in a pan, add the minced beef, chicken livers and bacon and fry until browned, stirring occasionally.
2. Add the onion, garlic, carrot and celery and fry for about 3 minutes, until softened.
3. Pour in the wine and cook for 3–5 minutes, until reduced by about half.
4. Stir in the stock, tomato purée, bay leaf, and plenty of nutmeg, salt and pepper. Bring to the boil, cover and simmer for 25–30 minutes.
5. Meanwhile, cook the pasta. Drain and toss in a little olive oil and add a little grated nutmeg and pepper.
6. Serve the sauce mixed in with the pasta, or separately. Hand the cheese separately, to sprinkle on top.

LASAGNE VERDI AL FORNO

Twice the quantity of Ragù (above)
8–10 sheets lasagne verdi, cooked
75 g (3 oz) Parmesan cheese, grated

BÉCHAMEL SAUCE:
50 g (2 oz) butter
75 g (3 oz) plain flour
1.2 litres (2 pints) hot milk
1 bay leaf
grated nutmeg, salt and pepper to taste

1. Make the ragù the day before required, if possible.
2. To make the sauce, melt the butter in a saucepan and stir in the flour. Cook for about 1 minute, then gradually stir in the hot milk, until smooth. Bring to the boil, stirring. Season well with nutmeg, salt and pepper, add the bay leaf and simmer for about 5 minutes. Remove the bay leaf.
3. Lightly grease a large shallow dish and fill with alternate layers of ragù, pasta and sauce, sprinkling each layer with grated Parmesan.
4. Bake in a preheated oven, 190°C/375°F/Gas Mark 5, for about 40 minutes, until the top is browned. Leave to stand for a few minutes before cutting.

Serves 6–8
Preparation time: 50 minutes, plus cooking ragù and pasta
Cooking time: About 40 minutes
Freezing: Recommended at end of stage 3

VARIATION
For a simpler supper-style lasagne, omit the ragù and substitute about 500 g (1 lb) cooked diced chicken, 125 g (4 oz) sliced button mushrooms, 125 g (4 oz) chopped ham and 2 tablespoons dry sherry: add to the sauce and arrange in layers with the pasta as above.

VEGETARIAN DISHES

CREAMY BEANS IN MUSHROOM CUPS

4 large flat mushrooms
oil for brushing
25 g (1 oz) butter
4 spring onions, chopped
2 tablespoons chopped
*   parsley*
1 teaspoon chopped dill

50 g (2 oz) cream cheese
*   or low-fat soft cheese*
150 ml (¼ pint) milk
125 g (4 oz) flageolet or
*   haricot beans, cooked*
salt and pepper to taste
dill sprigs to garnish

Serves 4
Preparation time:
10 minutes, plus
cooking beans
Cooking time:
10–15 minutes
Freezing:
Not recommended

1. Remove the stalks from the mushrooms, chop them finely and set aside.
2. Brush both sides of the mushroom cups with oil, place in a baking dish, and season with salt and pepper. Cover and cook in a preheated oven, 200°C/400°F/Gas Mark 6, for 10–15 minutes, until softened. Reserve any juices.
3. Meanwhile, melt the butter in a pan, add the spring onions and chopped mushroom stalks and sauté for about 5 minutes. Add any mushroom juices, the parsley, dill, and salt and pepper.
4. Add the cheese and milk and stir gently until melted and creamy. Stir in the beans and reheat.
5. Arrange the mushrooms on warmed individual plates and fill with the bean mixture. Garnish with dill to serve.

ADUKI BEAN BURGERS

250 g (8 oz) aduki beans,
*   cooked*
2 tablespoons oil
1 large onion, chopped
2 cloves garlic, crushed
1 teaspoon yeast extract
½ vegetable stock cube

75 g (3 oz) wholemeal
*   breadcrumbs*
wholemeal flour for
*   coating*
oil for shallow frying
salt and pepper to taste

Makes 8
Preparation time:
25 minutes, plus
cooking beans
Cooking time:
12 minutes
Freezing:
Recommended

1. Mash half of the beans, then mix in the rest.
2. Heat the oil in a pan, add the onion and garlic and fry for 5 minutes. Stir in the yeast extract and stock cube. Mix into the beans with the breadcrumbs, and salt and pepper.
3. With wet hands, form the mixture into 8 patties. Coat with flour and fry in the hot oil for 3 minutes on each side.
4. Serve in pitta bread with salad and relishes.

MIXED GRAIN CROQUETTES

This is a good way of using up leftover cooked grains. If possible, try to use home-sprouted beans (see page 8) —lentils are especially good.

1 tablespoon oil
1 onion, chopped finely
1 clove garlic, crushed
1/2 teaspoon curry powder
175 g (6 oz) mixed cooked grains, e.g. rice, millet, bulgur wheat, pearl barley
75 g (3 oz) bean sprouts, e.g. lentil, mung, aduki

75 g (3 oz) roasted peanuts, ground
50 g (2 oz) matured Cheddar cheese, grated
25 g (1 oz) self-raising flour
2 eggs, beaten
4 tablespoons milk
salt and pepper to taste
oil for deep-frying

Makes 16
Preparation time:
15 minutes
Cooking time:
20 minutes
Freezing:
Not recommended

1. Heat the oil in a pan, add the onion and garlic and fry for 5 minutes, then add the curry powder and fry for 1 minute. Leave to cool.
2. Stir in the remaining ingredients.
3. Drop a few dessertspoonfuls of the batter into hot oil and deep-fry for about 1½ minutes, until golden and crisp. Drain on kitchen paper. Repeat with the remaining batter. Serve piping hot as a light meal. Good with Tahini Cream (page 14).

STUFFED CABBAGE

A whole stuffed cabbage makes an impressive centrepiece as a main meatless meal. It is best made with a close-textured filling which will cut into wedges to serve.

1 primo or Savoy cabbage
25 g (1 oz) butter
1 onion, chopped
1 clove garlic, crushed
125 g (4 oz) red lentils
600 ml (1 pint) vegetable stock
1/2 teaspoon ground coriander

2 tablespoons each chopped parsley and dill
125 g (4 oz) long-grain rice, cooked
2 tablespoons pine nuts, toasted
75 g (3 oz) hard cheese, grated (optional)
1 egg, beaten
salt and pepper to taste

1. Remove any large loose outer leaves from the cabbage. Cut off the top of the cabbage, then remove the inside

leaves, leaving about a 2 cm (¾ inch) thickness all round. (Use the inner leaves for another dish.)

2. Steam or blanch the cabbage shell and its top for 5–10 minutes or until just softened but still firm. Cool and drain upside down.

3. Melt the butter in a pan, add the onion and garlic and fry gently for 5 minutes. Add the lentils, stock, coriander, herbs, and salt and pepper. Bring to the boil, then cover and simmer for about 15 minutes, until the liquid has been absorbed and the lentils are cooked.

4. Stir in the rice, pine nuts, reserving a few for garnish, and cheese, if using. Leave to cool for 5 minutes, then add the egg. Check the seasoning.

5. Spoon into the cabbage shell. Peel some leaves from the blanched top and place over the filling to enclose. Stand the cabbage on a large sheet of greased foil and wrap to enclose completely.

6. Steam for about 45 minutes, or until tender. Leave to stand for about 5 minutes, then unwrap and sprinkle with the remaining nuts. Serve with a sauce, such as Tomato Coulis (page 22), Cheese Sauce (page 54) or Lemon Sauce (page 48).

Serves 4–6
Preparation time: 45 minutes, plus cooking rice
Cooking time: 45 minutes
Freezing: Not recommended

STUFFED LEAVES WITH LEMON SAUCE

12 large chard or cabbage leaves	100 g (3½ oz) bulgur wheat
25 g (1 oz) butter	227 g (8 oz) pack low fat soft cheese
1 leek, chopped	salt and pepper to taste
1 carrot, chopped	lemon slices to garnish
125 g (4 oz) mushrooms, sliced thinly	FOR THE SAUCE:
600 ml (1 pint) vegetable stock	3 tablespoons plain flour
100 g (3½ oz) red lentils	150 ml (¼ pint) water
½ teaspoon dried thyme	juice of 1 lemon
	3 eggs, beaten

Serves 4–6
Preparation time:
40 minutes
Cooking time:
30 minutes–
1 hour
Freezing:
Recommended for
cabbage rolls only

1. Remove the thick ribs from the chard or cabbage leaves, forming a 'V' shape. Blanch the leaves in about 1 litre (1¾ pints) lightly salted water for 2–6 minutes, until softened. Drain, reserving the water, cool and lay out on a worktop.

2. Melt the butter in a pan, add the leek and carrot and fry for about 5 minutes, until softened. Add the mushrooms and cook for about 3 minutes.

3. Pour in three quarters of the stock and add the lentils, thyme, and salt and pepper. Bring to the boil, cover and simmer for about 10 minutes.

4. Meanwhile, soak the bulgur wheat in the remaining stock for 5 minutes. Stir into the lentil mixture with the cheese. Check the seasoning.

5. Spoon the filling onto the stalk end of the leaves. Fold the stalk ends over, then fold in the sides and roll up. Place in a roasting tin, join side down.

6. Pour over the reserved cabbage water, adding extra stock or water if the rolls are not covered. Season with salt and pepper, and cover with foil.

7. Bake in a preheated oven, 190°C/375°F/Gas Mark 5, for about 30 minutes for chard leaves and up to 1 hour for cabbage. Remove with a slotted spoon to a serving dish and keep warm. Strain 600 ml (1 pint) of the stock.

8. To make the sauce, blend the flour and water in a pan. Whisk in the reserved stock and bring to the boil, whisking until smooth. Add the lemon juice and cool slightly.

9. Put the eggs in a bowl, pour on a little stock, then return to the pan. On the lowest possible heat, stir until the sauce thickens then remove immediately; sometimes it thickens on mixing and does not need reheating.

10. Check the seasoning and pour over the stuffed rolls. Garnish with lemon slices to serve.

TAMALE PIE

This Mexican-style recipe is a bean and chilli pot topped with cornbread.

2 tablespoons oil
1 onion, chopped
1 clove garlic, crushed
¹/₂ green pepper, chopped
1 celery stick, chopped
¹/₂ teaspoon chilli powder
1 tablespoon tomato purée
397 g (14 oz) can chopped
*   tomatoes*
12 pitted green olives,
*   sliced*
75 g (3 oz) sweetcorn
*   kernels*
150 g (5 oz) red kidney
*   beans, cooked*

2 tablespoons chopped
*   parsley*
salt and pepper to taste
FOR THE TOPPING:
125 g (4 oz) cornmeal
1 tablespoon plain flour
¹/₂ teaspoon salt
2 teaspoons baking
*   powder*
1 egg, beaten
100 ml (3¹/₂ fl oz) milk
1 tablespoon oil
50 g (2 oz) Cheddar
*   cheese, grated*

Serves 4
Preparation time:
30 minutes, plus
cooking beans
Cooking time:
40–45 minutes
Freezing:
Recommended

1. Heat the oil in a large saucepan, add the onion, garlic, green pepper and celery and fry for about 10 minutes, until softened. Sprinkle in the chilli powder and cook for 1 minute. Season with salt and pepper.
2. Stir in the remaining ingredients, bring to the boil, then simmer for 5 minutes. Spoon into a greased 1.75 litre (3 pint) ovenproof pie dish.
3. Blend the cornmeal with the flour, salt and baking powder, then beat in the egg, milk and oil until smooth; the mixture should resemble a thick batter. Spoon over the bean mixture and sprinkle with the cheese.
4. Bake in a preheated oven, 220°C/425°F/Gas Mark 7, for 40–45 minutes, until golden and firm. Serve hot.

COURGETTE AND TOMATO DHAL

250 g (8 oz) yellow split
*   peas*
600 ml (1 pint) stock
1 onion, chopped
2 tablespoons oil
1 teaspoon black mustard
*   seeds*
2.5 cm (1 inch) piece fresh
*   root ginger, chopped*

1 clove garlic, crushed
¹/₂ green pepper, chopped
1 teaspoon turmeric
1 teaspoon garam masala
1 large courgette, sliced
2 large tomatoes, skinned
*   and chopped*
juice of ¹/₂ lemon
salt and pepper to taste

1. Place the split peas, stock, half of the onion, and salt in a saucepan. Cover, bring to the boil, then simmer for about 25 minutes, until the peas are soft but still whole.
2. Meanwhile, heat the oil in another pan, add the mustard seeds, cover and fry until they stop popping. Add the remaining onion, the ginger, garlic and green pepper and fry gently for 5 minutes.
3. Add the turmeric and garam masala and cook for 1 minute, then add the courgette, tomato, lemon juice, about 2 tablespoons water, and salt and pepper. Cover and simmer for 5 minutes.
4. Carefully mix the vegetables and split peas together and transfer to a warmed serving dish. If serving as a main dish, serve with boiled rice and halved hard-boiled eggs, or with naan bread or chapatis.

Serves 4
Preparation time:
20 minutes
Cooking time:
25 minutes
Freezing:
Recommended

VEGETABLE AND BEAN COUS COUS

500 g (1 lb) cous cous
2 tablespoons olive oil
25 g (1 oz) butter
1 large onion, sliced
1 clove garlic, crushed
2 carrots, sliced
250 g (8 oz) parsnips, diced
1 teaspoon each turmeric and ground coriander
125 g (4 oz) white beans, cooked

125 g (4 oz) button mushrooms
175 g (6 oz) French beans, halved
4 tomatoes, skinned and quartered
300 ml (1/2 pint) each vegetable stock and dry cider
6 canned artichoke hearts, halved
salt and pepper to taste

Serves 4–6
Preparation time:
30 minutes, plus cooking beans
Cooking time:
20 minutes
Freezing:
Not recommended

1. Prepare the cous cous according to packet instructions if easy-cook, or as for Cous Cous with Spiced Lamb (page 40).
2. Heat the oil and butter in a pan, add the onion, garlic, carrot and parsnip and fry gently for 10 minutes, or until softened. Sprinkle in the spices and cook for 1 minute.
3. Add the remaining ingredients, except the cous cous, and bring to the boil.
4. Put the cous cous into a steamer that fits on top of the saucepan, cover and simmer for about 20 minutes.
5. Serve the cous cous topped with the vegetables.

CHICK PEA AND CAULIFLOWER CURRY

2 tablespoons oil
2 cloves garlic, crushed
1–2 green chillies, seeded
  and sliced
2.5 cm (1 inch) piece fresh
  root ginger, grated
1 large onion, chopped
1 teaspoon each turmeric,
  paprika, ground
  coriander, and
  fenugreek seeds
2 teaspoons ground cumin
1/4 teaspoon cinnamon
1 tablespoon tomato purée

1 litre (1³/4 pints) vegetable
  stock
1 tablespoon lemon juice
250 g (8 oz) small
  potatoes, halved
1 small cauliflower,
  broken into florets
250 g (8 oz) chick peas,
  cooked
3 tablespoons natural
  yogurt
2 tablespoons desiccated
  coconut
salt and pepper to taste

1. Heat the oil in a pan, add the garlic, chillies, ginger and onion and fry for about 5 minutes. Add the spices and fry for 1–2 minutes, then add the tomato purée, stock, lemon juice, and salt and pepper and bring to the boil.

2. Add the potatoes, cover and cook for 5 minutes. Add the cauliflower and chick peas, cover and simmer for 15 minutes or until the potatoes are tender.

3. Add yogurt, top with coconut and serve with rice.

Serves 4
Preparation time:
20 minutes, plus
cooking chick peas
Cooking time:
25–30 minutes
Freezing:
Recommended

STUFFED SPINACH PANCAKES

If you prefer a lower fat dish, use skimmed milk and low fat cheese.

FOR THE PANCAKES:
125 g (4 oz) plain flour
1 large egg (size 1 or 2)
300 ml (½ pint) milk
125 g (4 oz) leaf spinach,
*   blanched, squeezed dry*
*   and chopped finely*
FOR THE FILLING:
1 tablespoon oil
1 onion, chopped
397 g (14 oz) can chopped
*   tomatoes*
2 tablespoons tomato
*   chutney or ketchup*
¼ teaspoon ground
*   cinnamon*

good pinch each of allspice
*   and ground cloves*
1 thyme sprig or ½
*   teaspoon dried thyme*
175 g (6 oz) red kidney,
*   pinto or borlotti beans,*
*   cooked*
FOR THE CHEESE SAUCE:
40 g (1½ oz) plain flour
40 g (1½ oz) butter
600 ml (1 pint) milk
125 g (4 oz) matured
*   Cheddar cheese, grated*
salt and pepper to taste

Serves 4
Preparation time:
20–25 minutes,
plus cooking
beans
Cooking time:
25 minutes
Freezing:
Recommended

1. First, prepare the filling. Heat the oil in a pan, add the onion and sauté for 5 minutes. Add the tomatoes, chutney or ketchup, spices, thyme, salt and pepper. Bring to the boil, add the beans, cover and simmer for 20 minutes.
2. Meanwhile, make the pancakes. Place all the ingredients in a blender or food processor and work until smooth. Alternatively, place the flour in a bowl and make a well in the centre. Add the egg and half of the milk and beat until smooth. Stir in the spinach and remaining milk.
3. Brush an omelette pan lightly with oil and place over a high heat until hot. Pour in just enough batter to cover the base thinly, tilting the pan. Cook until the edge is golden and bubbles appear on the surface. Turn with a palette knife and cook the other side until golden. Repeat with the remaining batter, to make 8 pancakes. Stack between sheets of greaseproof paper and keep warm.
4. To make the sauce, place the flour, butter and milk in a pan, bring to the boil, stirring until smooth and thickened, then simmer for 2 minutes. Remove from the heat and stir in three quarters of the cheese, and salt and pepper.
5. Divide the filling between the pancakes and roll up. Place in a shallow ovenproof dish, pouring some sauce in between and the rest over the top. Sprinkle with the remaining cheese and place under a preheated moderate grill until golden and bubbling. Serve with salad.

TAGLIATELLE IN MUSHROOM SAUCE

This sauce needs dried cèpes or porcini mushrooms to add a depth of flavour. They are expensive, but a small packet will be plenty as they swell on soaking.

*500 g (1 lb) fresh tagliatelle
 or 350 g (12 oz) dried
25 g (1 oz) dried
 mushrooms (see above)
25 g (1 oz) butter
1 small onion, chopped
250 g (8 oz) button
 mushrooms, sliced
3 tablespoons dry sherry*

*1 teaspoon chopped
 marjoram or oregano
142 ml (5 fl oz) carton
 single cream
50 g (2 oz) Parmesan
 cheese, grated
grated nutmeg, salt and
 pepper to taste*

1. Cook the pasta, then drain. Meanwhile, soak the dried mushrooms in boiling water to cover for 10 minutes. Drain, reserving the liquid, and slice.

2. Heat the butter in a pan, add the onion and sauté for 3 minutes. Add all the mushrooms, sherry, reserved liquid, herbs, and nutmeg, salt and pepper. Cover and simmer for 3 minutes, shaking the pan occasionally.

3. Stir in the cream and heat gently. Toss into the pasta, heat through then transfer to a warmed serving dish. Sprinkle with the cheese and serve immediately.

Serves 4
Preparation time:
10 minutes
Cooking time:
10–15 minutes
Freezing:
Not recommended

GARDENERS PIE

A 'Shepherds Pie' free of animal products, using soya beans as the main protein base and lots of tasty vegetables.

4 tablespoons oil
1 onion, chopped
2 cloves garlic, crushed
2 celery sticks, sliced
2 carrots, diced
1 large leek, sliced
125 g (4 oz) mushrooms, sliced
3 tomatoes, skinned and chopped
2–3 tablespoons wholemeal flour
600 ml (1 pint) vegetable stock

1 teaspoon yeast extract
125 g (4 oz) soya beans, cooked
2 thyme sprigs or ½ teaspoon dried thyme
1 teaspoon chopped marjoram
350 g (12 oz) potatoes, sliced very thinly
2 teaspoons sesame seeds or wholemeal breadcrumbs
salt and pepper to taste

Serves 4–6
Preparation time:
20 minutes, plus cooking beans
Cooking time:
40 minutes
Freezing:
Recommended

1. Heat half of the oil in a pan, add the onion, garlic, celery, carrot and leek and fry for about 10 minutes, until softened. Add the mushrooms and tomatoes and cook for 2 minutes.
2. Sprinkle in the flour, stir well, then add the stock and yeast extract. Bring to the boil, stirring, then add the beans, herbs, and salt and pepper. Spoon into a shallow casserole.
3. Arrange the potato on top, season with salt and pepper and brush with the remaining oil. Sprinkle with the sesame seeds or breadcrumbs.
4. Bake in a preheated oven, 190°C/375°F/Gas Mark 5, for 40 minutes, until the potatoes are browned. Serve hot.

LENTIL SOUFFLÉ WITH CROÛTES

2½ slices wholemeal bread, buttered
175 g (6 oz) red lentils
1 small onion, chopped finely
1 carrot, grated finely
600 ml (1 pint) vegetable stock or water
1 bay leaf
75 g (3 oz) matured Cheddar cheese, grated

75 g (3 oz) wholemeal breadcrumbs
2 eggs, separated
salt and pepper to taste
FOR THE MUSHROOM SAUCE:
25 g (1 oz) butter
125 g (4 oz) mushrooms, chopped finely
3 tablespoons plain flour
300 ml (½ pint) milk

1. Cut the bread into 10 triangles, discarding the crusts. Arrange, buttered sides outwards, around the side of a greased 20 cm (8 inch) flan dish.

2. Place the lentils, onion, carrot, stock or water, bay leaf, salt and pepper in a saucepan, bring to the boil, cover and simmer for 30 minutes. Remove the bay leaf.

3. Stir vigorously until the mixture is smooth. Reserve 2 tablespoons cheese and 1 tablespoon breadcrumbs; stir in the rest. Cool slightly, then beat in the egg yolks.

4. Whisk the egg whites until stiff, then fold in carefully. Turn into the prepared dish and sprinkle with the reserved cheese and breadcrumbs mixed together.

5. Bake in a preheated oven, 180°C/350°F/Gas Mark 4, for about 30 minutes, until golden, risen and firm.

6. Meanwhile, make the sauce. Melt the butter in a pan, add the mushrooms and sauté for 3 minutes. Stir in the flour and cook, stirring, for 2 minutes. Gradually add the milk, stirring until smooth and thickened. Season well with salt and pepper and simmer for 2 minutes.

7. Serve the soufflé immediately, with the sauce.

Serves 4
Preparation time:
45 minutes
Cooking time:
30 minutes
Freezing:
Not recommended

BEAN KOFTAS

Koftas, or Keftas, are North African spicy meat patties moulded around kebab sticks and grilled; this is a vegetarian version. They can be made ahead and stored chilled until ready to cook, but should be eaten as soon as they come out of the pan.

125 g (4 oz) bulgur wheat or millet
300 ml (½ pint) vegetable stock
2 tablespoons oil
125 g (4 oz) mushrooms, chopped finely
1 onion, chopped finely
2 cloves garlic, crushed
½ teaspoon ground coriander
1 teaspoon ground cumin
2 teaspoons paprika
125 g (4 oz) aduki beans, cooked until soft
1 tablespoon chopped mint
3 tablespoons chopped parsley

1 tablespoon chopped coriander (optional)
1 egg, beaten
wholemeal flour for coating
oil for shallow frying
salt and pepper to taste
FOR THE RAITA:
¼ cucumber, peeled, seeded and grated
2 spring onions, chopped
6 tablespoons natural yogurt
1 tablespoon chopped mint
TO GARNISH:
chicory leaves
watercress sprigs

Serves 4–6
Preparation time:
30 minutes, plus cooking beans and chilling
Cooking time:
20 minutes
Freezing:
Not recommended

1. Place the bulgur wheat or millet and stock in a pan, cover and cook for 5 minutes, until the liquid has been absorbed. Season well with salt and pepper. Set aside.
2. Heat the oil in a pan, add the mushrooms, onion and garlic, cover and cook gently for about 10 minutes, until soft. Add the spices and fry for 2 minutes.
3. Place in a blender or food processor with the beans, herbs, egg, and salt and pepper and work to a thick purée.
4. Mix with the bulgur wheat or millet in a bowl and chill for 1 hour.
5. Using wet hands, shape into small oval patties and toss in flour to coat. Heat the oil in a frying pan and shallow fry the patties in batches until crisp and golden on both sides, turning once or twice.
6. Meanwhile, mix together the ingredients for the raita and season with salt and pepper. Spoon into a small bowl.
7. Serve the koftas garnished with chicory and watercress, and accompanied by the raita.

MACARONI AND VEGETABLE PIE

25 g (1 oz) margarine
2 leeks, sliced
2 carrots, sliced
1 clove garlic, crushed
2 × 397 g (14 oz) cans
   plum tomatoes
2 oregano sprigs or 1
   teaspoon dried oregano
1 thyme sprig or ½
   teaspoon dried thyme

125 g (4 oz) red or white
   kidney beans, cooked
250 g (8 oz) macaroni,
   cooked
175 g (6 oz) Cheddar
   cheese, grated
2 eggs, beaten
4 tablespoons fresh
   breadcrumbs
salt and pepper to taste

Serves 4
Preparation time:
25 minutes, plus
cooking beans and
pasta
Cooking time:
30–35 minutes
Freezing:
Recommended

1. Melt the margarine in a pan, add the leeks, carrots and garlic, cover and cook gently until softened.
2. Add the tomatoes with their juice, herbs, and salt and pepper, and bring to the boil. Add the beans and simmer for 5 minutes.
3. Mix the vegetables with the pasta, add two thirds of the cheese and cool slightly. Stir in the eggs, then transfer to a large ovenproof dish.
4. Mix the remaining cheese with the breadcrumbs and sprinkle on top. Bake in a preheated oven, 190°C/375°F/Gas Mark 5, for 30–35 minutes, until crisp and golden. Leave to stand for a few minutes before serving.

SPAGHETTI SOUFFLÉ

50 g (2 oz) butter
40 g (1½ oz) plain flour
¼ teaspoon mustard
*   powder*
300 ml (½ pint) hot milk
75 g (3 oz) matured
*   Cheddar or Gruyère*
*   cheese, grated*

50 g (2 oz) Parmesan
*   cheese, grated*
3 eggs, separated
75 g (3 oz) dried spaghetti,
*   cooked and chopped*
*   roughly*
3 tablespoons dried
*   breadcrumbs*
salt and pepper to taste

1. Melt the butter in a pan, add the flour and mustard and cook, stirring, for 1 minute. Gradually stir in the milk until smooth. Simmer for 2 minutes.
2. Remove from the heat and stir in the cheeses, reserving 1 tablespoon Parmesan. Cool slightly, then beat in the egg yolks, spaghetti, and salt and pepper.
3. Brush the inside of a 1.2 litre (2 pint) soufflé dish with oil, then coat with the breadcrumbs.
4. Whisk the egg whites until stiff. Stir 1 tablespoon into the sauce to lighten, then fold in the rest. Spoon into the dish, sprinkle with the reserved Parmesan and bake in a preheated oven, 180°C/350°F/Gas Mark 4, for about 40 minutes, until risen and golden. Serve immediately.

Serves 3–4
Preparation time:
25 minutes, plus
cooking pasta
Cooking time:
40 minutes
Freezing:
Not recommended

SALADS

INDONESIAN HOT RICE SALAD

4 tablespoons sesame seed
 oil
juice of 2 limes or 1 lemon
1 clove garlic, crushed
2 dried red chillies, seeded
 and crushed
2 tablespoons soy sauce
1–2 teaspoons clear honey
2 tablespoons wine
 vinegar
350 g (12 oz) brown rice,
 cooked and hot
3 spring onions, sliced
 thinly
227 g (8 oz) can pineapple
 pieces in natural juice

250 g (8 oz) bean sprouts
 (preferably home
 sprouted)
2 celery sticks, sliced
50 g (2 oz) raisins
50 g (2 oz) unsalted
 peanuts
50 g (2 oz) cashew nuts,
 toasted (optional)
2 tablespoons sesame
 seeds, toasted
1 small red pepper, cored,
 seeded and sliced
salt and pepper to taste

Serves 6
Preparation time:
15 minutes, plus
cooking rice
Freezing:
Not recommended

1. Place the oil, lime or lemon juice, garlic, chillies, soy sauce, honey, vinegar, and salt and pepper in a large bowl and mix well.
2. Add the hot rice and remaining ingredients and mix well. Check the seasoning. Serve hot or cold.

BEAN SPROUT AND RICE SALAD

125 g (4 oz) long-grain
 rice, cooked and hot
2 spring onions, chopped
2 carrots, sliced thinly
125 g (4 oz) bean sprouts
 (preferably home
 sprouted)
2 bunches watercress

FOR THE DRESSING:
3 tablespoons lemon juice
1 teaspoon Dijon mustard
1 teaspoon sugar
4 tablespoons olive oil
2 tablespoons single cream
salt and pepper to taste

Serves 4
Preparation time:
20 minutes, plus
cooking rice
Freezing:
Not recommended

1. Mix the dressing ingredients together, then toss into the hot rice. Leave to cool.
2. Add the spring onions, carrots and bean sprouts and mix well. Check the seasoning.
3. Arrange the watercress around the edge of a serving platter and spoon the salad into the centre.

BROWN RICE SALAD WITH CHICORY

250 g (8 oz) brown rice,
cooked and hot
7.5 cm (3 inch) piece
cucumber
1 head chicory
2 hard-boiled eggs,
chopped
1 large carrot, grated
4 spring onions, chopped
8–12 black olives, pitted

FOR THE DRESSING:
4 tablespoons olive or
sunflower oil
2 tablespoons wine
vinegar
1 tablespoon freshly
squeezed orange juice
1 teaspoon clear honey
1 teaspoon coarse-grain
mustard
salt and pepper to taste

Serves 4
Preparation time:
20 minutes, plus
cooking rice
Freezing:
Not recommended

1. Mix together the dressing ingredients, then toss into the hot rice. Leave to cool.
2. Quarter the cucumber lengthways, discard the seeds, then slice thinly.
3. Cut off the tips halfway down the chicory head and set aside for garnish. Slice the stem into rings.
4. Add the cucumber, chicory and remaining ingredients to the rice and toss well. Check the seasoning.
5. Line the edge of a shallow dish with the chicory tips and pile the salad into the centre to serve.

BEAN AND TUNA SALAD

An ideal salad to serve as a summer buffet dish.

*125 g (4 oz) white kidney
    beans, cooked and hot
6 anchovy fillets
2 celery sticks, sliced
8 stuffed olives, sliced
198 g (7 oz) can tuna,
    drained and flaked
FOR THE DRESSING:
1 teaspoon Dijon mustard
2 tablespoons tarragon
    vinegar
1 clove garlic, crushed*

*4 tablespoons olive oil
2 tablespoons chopped
    parsley
1 tablespoon snipped
    chives
1 teaspoon each chopped
    tarragon and marjoram
salt and pepper to taste
TO GARNISH:
4–6 quails eggs,
    hard-boiled and halved*

1. Mix the dressing ingredients together in a large bowl, add the hot beans and toss gently. Cool and chill.
2. Chop 3 anchovy fillets. Cut the rest in half lengthways and set aside for garnish.
3. Add the chopped anchovies, celery, olives and tuna to the beans and mix well. Check the seasoning.
4. Pile the salad onto a platter and garnish with the reserved anchovy strips and quails eggs to serve.

Serves 4–6
Preparation time:
20 minutes, plus cooking beans
Freezing:
Not recommended

THREE BEAN AND NUT SALAD

75 g (3 oz) pinto, red
  kidney or borlotti beans
75 g (3 oz) white
  cannellini beans
125 g (4 oz) French beans,
  quartered
1 small bulb fennel, sliced
  thinly
1 tablespoon oil
75 g (3 oz) sweetcure
  streaky bacon, derinded
  and diced
2 tablespoons red wine or
  raspberry vinegar

50 g (2 oz) walnuts,
  almonds or cashew
  nuts
FOR THE DRESSING:
1 teaspoon coarse-grain
  mustard
3 tablespoons finely
  chopped onion
2 tablespoons red wine
  vinegar
2 tablespoons olive oil
$1/2$ teaspoon salt
black pepper to taste

Serves 4
Preparation time:
15 minutes, plus
cooking beans
Freezing:
Not recommended

1. Cook the dried beans until tender; drain.
2. Blanch the French beans for 2 minutes; drain.
3. Combine the dressing ingredients in a large salad bowl. Add the beans while still hot and toss gently. Mix in the fennel.
4. Heat the oil in a pan, add the bacon and fry until crisp. Remove with a slotted spoon and set aside.
5. Pour the vinegar into the pan and scrape up any sediment. Heat gently, then pour onto the beans, stirring to coat.
6. Sprinkle the nuts and bacon over the salad and serve immediately.

TACO CHILLI BEAN SALAD

1 tablespoon oil
250 g (8 oz) ground beef
  or minced pork
1 clove garlic, crushed
125 g (4 oz) can green
  chillies in brine, drained
  and chopped
397 g (14 oz) can chopped
  tomatoes
125 g (4 oz) red kidney
  beans, cooked
1 small Iceberg, Webbs or
  Cos lettuce

1 small onion, sliced
1 small green pepper,
  cored, seeded and sliced
75 g (3 oz) matured
  Cheddar cheese, grated
  (optional)
50 g (2 oz) taco shells or
  tortilla chips, broken
  roughly
salt and pepper to taste
1 tomato, cut into wedges,
  to garnish

1. Heat the oil in a frying pan, add the meat and garlic and fry until browned.

2. Add the chillies, tomatoes, beans, and salt and pepper, cover and simmer for 15 minutes. Uncover and continue cooking for 15 minutes.

3. Meanwhile, prepare the salad. Tear the lettuce into small pieces and place in a bowl. Mix in the onion, green pepper, cheese if using, and taco or tortilla pieces.

4. Pile the hot meat mixture into the centre and serve immediately, or allow the meat to get cold and then add to the salad. Garnish with tomato to serve.

Serves 4
Preparation time:
15 minutes, plus
cooking beans
Cooking time:
35 minutes
Freezing:
Recommended for
meat mixture only

TURKEY CORONATION SALAD

This is an adaptation of the famous dish served at the Coronation of 1952 and offered in various guises at celebrations ever since. It could be a main course salad, or one of several at a cold buffet.

350 g (12 oz) pasta shapes
3 tablespoons French dressing
75 g (3 oz) dried apricots, chopped
125 g (4 oz) black grapes, halved and seeded
2 celery sticks, sliced
1 green pepper, cored, seeded and sliced
50 g (2 oz) hazelnuts, cashew nuts, almonds or walnuts, toasted
750 g (1½ lb) cooked turkey meat, diced
salt and pepper to taste

FOR THE SAUCE:
2 tablespoons olive oil
1 onion, chopped
1 tablespoon mild curry powder
2 teaspoons tomato purée
2 tablespoons lemon or lime juice
2 tablespoons port or sweet sherry
300 ml (½ pint) mayonnaise
150 g (5.3 oz) carton natural yogurt
TO SERVE:
lettuce or endive leaves

Serves 6–8
Preparation time:
40 minutes, plus chilling
Cooking time:
About 10 minutes
Freezing:
Not recommended

1. Cook the pasta, drain and toss in the French dressing. Season well with salt and pepper. Leave to cool.
2. Meanwhile soak the apricots in hot water to cover for 20 minutes.
3. Set aside a few grapes for garnish. Place the rest in a large bowl with the celery, green pepper, nuts, turkey and pasta.
4. To make the sauce, heat the oil in a pan, add the onion and fry gently for about 5 minutes, until softened. Add the curry powder and fry for 1 minute.
5. Add the tomato purée, lemon or lime juice, port or sherry, apricots and their soaking water. Bring to the boil, season well with salt and pepper, then simmer for 2 minutes. Leave to cool completely.
6. Combine the curry sauce with the mayonnaise and yogurt, then stir into the salad ingredients. Check the seasoning. Chill for about 4 hours; if the mixture thickens add a little extra mayonnaise thinned with yogurt.
7. Line a salad bowl or large platter with lettuce or endive, spoon the salad into the centre and garnish with the reserved grapes. Serve with a tomato salad.

ACCOMPANIMENTS

MILD CURRY SPICE PILAF

2 tablespoons oil
1 onion, chopped
250 g (8 oz) long-grain
   rice
1 teaspoon turmeric
1/2 teaspoon ground
   coriander
pinch of ground cloves

600 ml (1 pint) light stock
   or water
1 bay leaf
15 g (1/2 oz) butter
salt and pepper to taste
lemon slices and parsley to
   garnish

Serves 4
Preparation time:
10 minutes
Cooking time:
20 minutes
Freezing:
Recommended

1. Heat the oil in a large pan, add the onion and fry until softened. Add the rice and fry for about 2 minutes, until it turns opaque.
2. Sprinkle in the spices and fry for 1 minute. Pour in the stock or water, add the bay leaf, and salt and pepper.
3. Bring to the boil, cover and simmer for 15 minutes or until the rice is tender. Fork through and stir in the butter. Garnish with lemon and parsley to serve.

ARROZ VERDE

From Central America, this rice dish will be popular with those who enjoy the flavour of green peppers. Serve it with grilled meats or fish.

3 tablespoons oil
2 green peppers, cored,
   seeded and chopped
1 large green chilli, seeded
   and chopped
3 spring onions, chopped
1 clove garlic, crushed
6 tablespoons chopped
   parsley

250 g (8 oz) long-grain
   rice
600 ml (1 pint) vegetable
   stock or water
salt and pepper to taste
2 hard-boiled eggs,
   quartered, to garnish

Serves 4
Preparation time:
15 minutes
Cooking time:
About 20 minutes
Freezing:
Recommended,
without the eggs

1. Heat the oil in a large pan, add the peppers, chilli, spring onion and garlic and fry until softened.
2. Add the remaining ingredients, bring to the boil, cover and simmer for 15 minutes or until the rice is tender.
3. Fork the rice through and pile into a warmed serving dish. Arrange the eggs on top to serve.

SAFFRON AND GINGER PILAF

An aromatic special rice, with an unusual crunch of fried vermicelli—ideal for entertaining.

pinch of saffron threads
1 tablespoon oil
25 g (1 oz) butter
1 onion, chopped
1 clove garlic, crushed
2.5 cm (1 inch) piece fresh
  root ginger, chopped

250 g (8 oz) long-grain
  rice, preferably Basmati
600 ml (1 pint) vegetable
  stock or water
25 g (1 oz) vermicelli
salt and pepper to taste

Serves 4–6
Preparation time:
30 minutes
Cooking time:
25 minutes
Freezing:
Recommended

1. Soak the saffron in a little boiling water for 30 minutes.
2. Heat the oil and half of the butter in a large pan, add the onion, garlic and ginger and fry for about 3 minutes, until softened.
3. Add the rice, fry for 7 minutes, stirring occasionally, then add the stock, saffron and liquid, salt and pepper. Bring to the boil, cover and simmer for 15 minutes.
4. Meanwhile, break up the vermicelli and fry in the remaining butter until brown, but not burnt.
5. Fork up the cooked rice and gently stir in the vermicelli or sprinkle it over the top to serve.

FRIED RICE

Fried rice is made with ready-cooked rice, unlike a pilaf in which the rice is fried before cooking. This makes it ideal for using with leftovers. Note that you will need to double the quantity of rice if weighing it after cooking. Add any of the ingredients listed opposite.

2 tablespoons oil
1 clove garlic, crushed
3 spring onions, chopped
125 g (4 oz) long-grain
  rice, cooked
1 tablespoon soy sauce

1 tablespoon mushroom
  ketchup
salt and pepper to taste
TO SERVE:
1 teaspoon sesame oil
shredded spring onion

Serves 4
Preparation time:
5 minutes, plus
cooking rice
Cooking time:
5 minutes
Freezing:
Not recommended

1. Heat the oil in a large frying pan or wok, add the garlic and spring onion and stir-fry for about 30 seconds. Add the rice and stir-fry until coated in the oil.
2. Stir in the soy sauce, mushroom ketchup, and salt and pepper. Heat through for a few minutes, until very hot. Serve sprinkled with sesame oil and spring onion.

VARIATIONS

Add 2 or 3 of the following to the fried rice, up to a total weight of 250 g (8 oz) so that they remain in proportion to the rice: chopped cooked chicken, pork or ham; prawns; mushrooms; cashew nuts or almonds; peas; sliced mange-touts; sliced waterchestnuts; bean sprouts; firm scrambled egg; broccoli, cabbage or beans.

Include 1 teaspoon chopped fresh root ginger, a pinch of 5-spice powder, or 1–2 tablespoons dry sherry if you wish.

CARDAMOM RICE

Cardamom is a popular rice spice in the East. It is something of an acquired taste, so try it in small amounts at first. Leave the pods whole if you want a subtle flavour, or break them open and crush the seeds with a rolling pin if you want a stronger flavour.

25 g (1 oz) butter
1 tablespoon oil
1 small onion, chopped
1 clove garlic, crushed
250 g (8 oz) long-grain rice
1 teaspoon mild curry powder
¼ teaspoon cinnamon
¼ teaspoon ground cumin
600 ml (1 pint) vegetable stock or water

2 tablespoons lemon juice
1 bay leaf
3 cardamom pods
50 g (2 oz) raisins
1 tablespoon blanched almonds, halved
2 tablespoons unsalted peanuts
1 tablespoon cashew nuts
salt and pepper to taste
coriander leaves or parsley sprigs to garnish

Serves 4–6
Preparation time:
15 minutes
Cooking time:
20 minutes
Freezing:
Recommended

1. Heat the butter and oil in a large pan, add the onion and garlic and fry for about 3 minutes. Add the rice and fry, stirring occasionally, until opaque.
2. Add the curry, cinnamon and cumin and fry for 1 minute, then pour in the stock or water, and lemon juice. Add the bay leaf, cardamom, raisins, salt and pepper. Bring to the boil, then cover and simmer for about 15 minutes.
3. Meanwhile, spread the nuts in a grill pan and toast until golden, stirring occasionally.
4. Remove the bay leaf and cardamom pods, if used whole, and stir in the nuts. Garnish with coriander or parsley and serve hot as an accompaniment to grilled meats, fish or kebabs.

BULGUR WHEAT AND LENTIL PILAF

250 g (8 oz) bulgur wheat
1.2 litres (2 pints) vegetable stock or water
2 tablespoons oil
1 onion, chopped
1 small green pepper, cored, seeded and chopped

2 celery sticks, chopped
2 carrots, chopped
½ teaspoon each ground coriander and cumin
125 g (4 oz) green lentils
2 bay leaves
salt and pepper to taste
chopped parsley to garnish

1. Place the bulgur wheat and half of the stock or water in a pan, bring to the boil, cover and simmer for 5 minutes, until the liquid is absorbed.

2. Spread out on a baking sheet and place in a preheated oven, 190°C/375°F/Gas Mark 5, for about 25 minutes, forking through twice to separate the grains.

3. Meanwhile, heat the oil in a pan, add the vegetables and fry for 5 minutes. Add the spices and cook for 1 minute.

4. Add the lentils, remaining stock or water, bay leaves, and salt and pepper. Bring to the boil, cover and simmer for 30 minutes, until the lentils are soft but still holding their shape. Remove the bay leaves.

5. Spoon the bulgur wheat onto a serving platter and top with the lentils. Sprinkle with parsley to serve.

Serves 4–6
Preparation time:
10 minutes
Cooking time:
35 minutes
Freezing:
Recommended

BUTTER BEANS WITH HERBS

Although very versatile, I think butter beans are best served with a creamy sauce. Low fat soft cheese melts easily and provides creaminess without excessive calories. Use only fresh herbs for this dish—a small pack of mixed herbs would be just right.

*½ × 150 g (6 oz) pack
low fat soft cheese
6 tablespoons milk
125 g (4 oz) butter beans,
cooked
3 tablespoons chopped
parsley*

*3 thyme sprigs, chopped
2 tablespoons snipped
chives
2 small sage leaves,
chopped
salt and pepper to taste
thyme sprigs to garnish*

Serves 4–6
Preparation time:
5 minutes, plus
cooking beans
Cooking time:
5 minutes
Freezing:
Recommended

1. Place the cheese and milk in a pan and heat gently, stirring until melted and smooth.
2. Add the beans, stirring gently to coat in the sauce. Stir in the herbs and season well with salt and pepper. Serve immediately, garnished with thyme.

BEANS WITH LETTUCE AND DILL

We're rather timid about cooking with lettuce in this country, perhaps thinking that it cooks away to nothing. In fact, it has a good texture, and it imparts a lovely flavour to the other ingredients.

*25 g (1 oz) butter or
margarine
1 small round lettuce,
shredded
1 leek, sliced
150 ml (¼ pint) vegetable
stock or water
1 teaspoon chopped dill*

*2 tablespoons chopped
parsley
125 g (4 oz) red or white
kidney beans, cooked
4 tablespoons single cream
grated nutmeg, salt and
pepper to taste*

Serves 4
Preparation time:
10 minutes, plus
cooking beans
Cooking time:
10 minutes
Freezing:
Not recommended

1. Melt the butter or margarine in a pan, add the lettuce and leek, and cook for about 5 minutes.
2. Add the stock or water, herbs, beans, and nutmeg, salt and pepper. Cover and simmer for 5 minutes.
3. Add the cream and stir carefully to blend. Reheat, but do not allow to boil. Serve hot.

BEAN GUMBO

Gumbos are American stews containing okra. Here I have
added beans to make a delicious side dish.

2 tablespoons oil
1 large onion, sliced
1 clove garlic, crushed
½ small green pepper,
* sliced*
250 g (8 oz) okra, sliced
* into chunks*
1 tablespoon chopped basil

397 g (14 oz) can chopped
* tomatoes*
150 ml (¼ pint) vegetable
* stock or water*
125 g (4 oz) black eye
* beans, cooked*
salt and pepper to taste

Serves 4–6
Preparation time:
5 minutes, plus
cooking beans
Cooking time:
20 minutes
Freezing:
Recommended

1. Heat the oil in a pan, add the onion, garlic and pepper
and fry for about 5 minutes. Add the remaining ingredients, except the beans.
2. Bring to the boil, then simmer for 10 minutes. Add the
beans and cook for 5 minutes. Serve hot.

PASTA WITH CARROTS AND THYME

250 g (8 oz) pasta shapes
500 g (1 lb) carrots, cut
*   into chunks or sticks*
25 g (1 oz) butter
4 spring onions, chopped
150 ml (1/4 pint) vegetable
*   stock or water*
150 ml (1/4 pint) dry cider

1 teaspoon clear honey
3 thyme sprigs or
*   1 teaspoon dried thyme*
2 tablespoons chopped
*   parsley*
juice of 1/2 lemon
salt and pepper to taste
chopped parsley to garnish

Serves 4–6
Preparation time:
10 minutes
Cooking time:
About 10 minutes
Freezing:
Not recommended

1. Cook the pasta. Meanwhile place all the remaining ingredients in a saucepan, cover and cook for 5–10 minutes, until the carrots are tender.

2. Drain the pasta, toss into the carrot mixture and serve hot, sprinkled with parsley.

PASTA WITH RATATOUILLE

This can be served as an accompaniment to meat, fish or other vegetables, or as a light meal in itself topped with grated cheese or served with poached eggs. Particularly nice made with wholewheat pasta.

1 small aubergine
1 large courgette
250 g (8 oz) pasta shapes
3 tablespoons olive oil
1 onion, sliced
1 clove garlic, crushed
1 red or green pepper,
*   cored, seeded and sliced*

397 g (14 oz) can chopped
*   tomatoes*
1 teaspoon Herbes de
*   Provence or mixed dried*
*   herbs*
salt and pepper to taste

Serves 4–6
Preparation time:
25 minutes
Cooking time:
10 minutes
Freezing:
Recommended

1. Cut the aubergine and courgette into fingers about 1 cm (1/2 inch) thick. Place the aubergine in a colander and sprinkle lightly with salt. Leave to drain for about 20 minutes, then rinse well and pat dry with kitchen paper.

2. Cook the pasta.

3. Meanwhile, heat 2 tablespoons of the oil in a pan, add the onion and garlic and fry gently for about 3 minutes. Add the pepper, courgette and aubergine, cover and cook for 3 minutes.

4. Add the tomatoes, herbs, and salt and pepper. Cover and cook for 3 minutes.

5. Drain the pasta, toss in the remaining oil, then add to the ratatouille. Serve hot or cold.

INDEX

Photography by: Roger Phillips
Designed by: Sue Storey
Home economist: Carole Handslip
Stylist: Gina Carminati
Illustration by: Linda Smith
Typeset by Rowland Phototypesetting Ltd